WHAT PEOPLE ARE SAYIN
AND *DIVINE I*

Whatever's holding you back will hold you back no more! In *Divine Intentions*, Doug Reed leaves no stone unturned! You will be changed, healed, and empowered to live out God's divine plan for your life!

—*Darryl Strawberry*
Evangelist and four-time World Series champion
New York Times best-selling author, *Finding My Way*

Divine Intentions is a powerful scriptural attestation that we are God's creative handiwork. This soul-stirring intimation reminds us that we have been personally called on a redemptive journey to an abundant life beyond our wildest dreams.

—*Rob Hoskins*
President, OneHope
Senior advisor, World Evangelical Alliance

Doug invites you on a compelling journey toward the life God intended you to live. *Divine Intentions* will touch your heart and mind as it connects you with the God who rescues, restores, relabels, and redirects your life. It's a captivating and life-transforming read.

—*David Brakke*
Pacific Northwest church planter and lead pastor
The Church at Maltby-Monroe, Maltby, WA

Divine Intentions charts a course for smoother sailing in life. While God is always our "Captain," Doug Reed puts inspirational wind in our sails with strategic concepts to stay on course.

—*Mark Alford*
News anchor, Fox4 News, Kansas City; fledgling sailor

A powerful compass leading you to true spiritual freedom! Doug Reed's *Divine Intentions* is a *must* for anyone longing to know *why* they're on this planet and *how* to become exactly *who* God made them to be.

—*Jesse Quiroz*
Lead pastor, *Journey Church*, Troy, MO

The first time I met Doug, we hiked up a mountain together. On that journey, I learned about Doug's passion for helping others find the freedom and purpose God has for them. This book is a great reflection of that passion. Get ready to take your own exciting journey as you read this book.

—*Joel Malm*
Founder, Summit Leaders; author, *Fully You*

The personal experiences shared by Pastor Doug Reed in *Divine Intentions* will impact people everywhere. New believers' and mature believers' faith will be strengthened. You will be motivated to do great exploits for the Lord.

—*Bishop Michael Grant*
First presiding bishop, Assemblies of God, Jamaica

In *Divine Intentions*, Doug Reed takes you by the hand and gently and biblically leads you from a place of pain to a place of healing and wholeness. A must read!

—*Rick Welborne*
Lead pastor, Life Church, Fruitland Park, FL

Doug not only believes the content that he has masterfully crafted for us in *Divine Intentions*, but he authentically lives it. Doug's insights on God's purpose, God's healing power, and God's direction are applicable for individuals or groups at all levels!

—*Nik Adwalpalker*
Lead pastor, Throggs Neck Community Church, Bronx, NY

Doug Reed is the clearest, most powerful voice on *restoration* to our generation. *Divine Intentions* brings this voice—and God's restoring power—to your easy chair.

—*Tim Enloe*
International conference speaker and author

Divine Intentions is a must read for anyone who desires to discover their own story that has been authored before the foundations of the earth.

—*Steve Lummer*
Lead pastor, Discovery Church, Prescott, AZ

Divine Intentions is an invitation to hope, healing, and the fulfilled life you long for. Caution: pick this book up and you won't put it down.

—*Paul Feuerstein*
Lead pastor, Helena First Church, Helena, MT

Doug Reed, in his book *Divine Intentions*, takes you down the road to self-worth and value—not through your eyes, but through the eye of your Creator. God has a plan. Even when you reach a dead end, He is there to build a new road.

—*Reggie Dabbs*
Motivational speaker and author, *Just Keep Breathing*

Doug has always had a passion to help people reach their full potential in God. Through this excellent, practical, and inspiring book, you will find yourself desiring to take the next step in discovering and living out God's personal purpose for you.

—*Jason St. John*
Lead pastor, Evangel Church, Kansas City, MO

Doug is a gift to the kingdom of God and to the church. He has been such a blessing to our church as we have partnered for kingdom work. I know you will be blessed by his heart and insights.

—*Chad Benson*
Lead and founding pastor, Lifegate Church, Burleson, TX

In *Divine Intentions*, Doug Reed brilliantly addresses the root issues that interrupt individuals (and families), keeping them from experiencing the life God intended. Whether you are looking to reset the course of your life or simply need a recalibration, this book will redirect you into God's purpose.

—*Alan Biggers*
Family specialist, pastor, and executive director
Teen Challenge Southeast, Kansas City Girls Academy

Doug has spoken into so many lives over the years and has helped changed the trajectory of hearts all over world. With this book, you get to experience his heart and what I have experienced by being around him. *Divine Intentions* will introduce you to what so many of us have been recipients of.

—*Terry Kelley*
Lead worship and production pastor, Hope Fellowship, Frisco, TX

DIVINE
INTENTIONS

DIVINE
INTENTIONS

The Life You're Supposed to Live,
The Person God Meant You to Be

DOUG K. REED

WHITAKER
HOUSE

DIVINE INTENTIONS
The Life You're Supposed to Live, The Person God Meant You to Be

Partnership International
705B SE Melody Ln, #308
Lee's Summit, MO 64063
pitrips.com
dougkreed.com

ISBN: 978-1-64123-388-0 • eBook ISBN: 978-1-64123-389-7
Printed in the United States of America
© 2020 by Doug K. Reed

Whitaker House
1030 Hunt Valley Circle • New Kensington, PA 15068
www.whitakerhouse.com

Library of Congress Cataloging-in-Publication Data
Names: Reed, Doug, 1968- author.
Title: Divine intentions : the life you're supposed to live, the person God
   meant you to be / Doug K. Reed.
Description: New Kensington : Whitaker House, 2020. | Summary: "Takes
   readers on a journey of self-discovery using four concepts (rescued,
   restored, relabeled, and redirected) with the aim of healing from soul
   wounds and transforming their lives"—Provided by publisher.
Identifiers: LCCN 2019038437 (print) | LCCN 2019038438 (ebook) | ISBN
   9781641233880 (trade paperback) | ISBN 9781641233897 (ebook)
Subjects: LCSH: Christian life.
Classification: LCC BV4501.3 .R4327 2020 (print) | LCC BV4501.3 (ebook) |
   DDC 248.4—dc23
LC record available at https://lccn.loc.gov/2019038437
LC ebook record available at https://lccn.loc.gov/2019038438

1 2 3 4 5 6 7 8 9 10 11 ⨆ 27 26 25 24 23 22 21 20

DEDICATION

I dedicate this book to my Savior.
When I was lost, You rescued me.
When I was labeled, You renamed me.
When I was broken, You restored me.
When I was drifting, You redirected me.

*For we are God's masterpiece. He has created us anew in Christ
Jesus, so we can do the good things he planned for us long ago.*
—Ephesians 2:20 (NLT)

CONTENTS

FOREWORD

I hope you are ready to begin living out the life you were truly created to live. That's why you have this book in your hands. You know there is more. You feel it deep down. The problem is that in some way, you feel stuck or at a crossroads.

I believe it is God's divine timing and plan for you to encounter the *Divine Intentions* He has laid out for you. Your story was written by a God who saw you before you were born, a God who loves you and has an adventure ready for you to live. Your story is connected to *His* story. Psalm 139:16 reminds us that *"every day of my life was recorded in your book. Every moment was laid out before a single day had passed."* God has a unique story that He has written just for you—one of purpose and calling, one that will have you making a difference for the glory of the Author, God Himself, the Creator of all.

The problem is, life happens. Mistakes are made. Hurt is inflicted. Detours take over and we get stuck between the life we are living and the life God intended for us to live. *Divine Intentions* will be your GPS and compass to get you back to the life you were created to live. It will take you through a four-step discovery process to help you become the person God meant for you to be.

This is more than a book by Doug Reed; it's his life message that I've seen him live out for years. I've seen countless people cross paths with

Doug and this message—and it altered the course of their lives. All over the world, there are men and women living out their stories for God as missionaries, authors, pastors, business leaders, parents, and more. They are changing the world as they live out their calling. They all have one thing in common: they were at a crossroads in their lives...and came across this life message under the ministry of Doug Reed. It changed who they were and what they would become.

There is one story in particular that stands out for me. Her story started out like so many do, full of hope and promise of a bright future designed by God. The problem is, she never knew about a God who loved her and created an adventurous story uniquely for her. She wasn't raised in church at all. Her parents were divorced before she hit her critical teen years. Like many others, she encountered abuse of every kind, along with an often-absent alcoholic father. This was her normal. She knew nothing else. Hurt was common. She thought life was about abuse and being de-valued. She didn't know of a greater love or a divine plan until she was in high school, when she was invited for the first time to a local church youth ministry meeting.

She had never been to church and was not aware of the gospel story. She didn't know about the heavenly Father who wanted to *rescue* her from the hurt and abuse she was accustomed to and *restore* her back to the person she was created to be. She didn't know the heavenly Father who wanted to *relabel* her as the gifted, powerful, and beautiful daughter of God that she was, who wanted to *redirect* her life to one of purpose so she would make a difference in her own future family and minister to thousands of others.

The offer of free pizza and a fun night got her into that church on a Wednesday night...but it was the life-changing message from the youth pastor that God used to open her heart.

Four years later, when she graduated from high school, she was a faith-ful member of the church's student ministry. She headed to Bible college to purse the ministry calling that she discovered was part of her divine story.

That girl was my wife, Kelly, the love of my life, who I met at that same Bible college. The youth minister, of course, was Pastor Doug Reed.

Doug became Kelly's spiritual father and I had to win him over to marry her. He officiated at our wedding and was an early mentor for us both when it came to ministry. Twenty years later, we are now best of friends and ministry partners. Kelly and I planted Destination Church in Virginia in 2011 and Doug has been part of our church story from the beginning. He now serves as our partnership/teaching pastor as well. I get to see the same life-changing message that changed my wife's story change the stories of thousands in our church. Besides speaking at our church several times a year, Doug travels across the country, sharing his message of God's restorative plan in churches and conferences. He also leads mission trips all over the world.

I am so excited to see the impact *Divine Intentions* will have on people's lives as they read and discover the four keys of being *rescued, restored, relabeled,* and *redirected.* I will be forever grateful for the ministry and friendship I've been honored to have with Doug. And I believe that after you see what this book does for your journey, you will be forever grateful, too. Get ready to live the life you're supposed to live, to become the person God meant for you to be. Enjoy discovering the *Divine Intentions* God has for you! *The best is yet to come.*

—*Bryan Briggs*
Lead pastor
Destination Church, Central Virginia

INTRODUCTION:
THE AUTHOR OF YOUR STORY

Looking unto Jesus, the author and finisher of our faith.
—Hebrews 12:2 NKJV

Your story began before you were even born. Your parents were chosen without your consent. Your family history was established before you took your first breath. Your personality, body type, and unique gifts were embedded in your DNA without any prior authorization from you. But none of it was haphazard.

Every story requires an *author* and your personal narrative is no exception. Your story has a divine Author who would be thrilled if you fulfilled the role He has planned for you. You existed in His loving, wildly creative imagination before you appeared on earth. In fact, you have been on His mind and in His heart for all eternity. His plans are perfect and His thoughts about you are not limited by time, space, or circumstance.

It can be hard to process this truth because our lives are far from perfect. But there is power and comfort knowing that He has a strategy for your story. Knowing that a better plan exists than the one you've been following is a starting point for revolutionary change in your life.

King David passionately crafted these words:

*You created my inmost being; you knit me together in my mother's womb. I praise you because I am fearfully and wonderfully made....
Your eyes saw my unformed body; all the days ordained for me were written in your book before one of them came to be.*

(Psalm 139:13–14, 16 NIV)

God has a book—and you and I are in it. All of David's days, your days, and my days are written in God's book. He started to write about us before we were even conceived!

However, the life we are living may not be the one He intended. In our hearts, we know this must be true because Jesus promised us an abundant life (see John 10:10) but few of us have that. Most of us have simply chosen a different life for ourselves, or we follow a path that someone else put before us. Most are not living the life God intended them to live.

Yet God is obsessed with us. He cares more about you than you care about yourself. The apostle Paul wrote, "*We are God's masterpiece. He has created us anew in Christ Jesus, so we can do the good things he planned for us long ago*" (Ephesians 2:10).

Think about it: you're a *masterpiece*. I used to think I was an accident, an experiment gone wrong, but then, I met the Author of my story and learned His plans for me. The chaos that I had made of my life had not nullified His creative work. And He didn't mind doing some rewriting! My mess could stop Him from crafting a masterpiece.

THE POWER TO FULFILL YOUR STORY

Let's pretend that I'm sitting down to write a book about *you*. I can make you rich or poor, plain or amazingly attractive. I could make you a person of influence, or a virtual nobody. I could write about you in a way that makes you struggle, or I could make you blessed beyond measure. Just one tiny problem: my book is *fictional*! I have no power to make the story come true. My authority as the author of your story ends quickly. Fantasy over. My point is, I don't have the power to make my vision of you come true—but God does. He is *"the author and finisher of our faith"* (Hebrews 12:2 NKJV).

YOUR DIVINE AUTHOR HAS WRITTEN ABOUT YOU
WITH A STRATEGIC, RECKLESS ABANDONMENT,
NEVER STOPPING TO CALCULATE THE COST OF
WHAT HE IS PROPOSING.

And God writes with a full creative freedom that has no limits. Your divine Author has written about you with a strategic, reckless abandonment, never stopping to calculate the cost of what He is proposing. When God planned your perfect reality in this world, He had *"glorious, unlimited resources"* (Ephesians 3:16) at His disposal. God desires to make His every plan and every purpose be your true-life story. His love for you is vast and He wants you to experience all that He has designed for you.

Unlike a story I might attempt to write about you, God's story isn't fiction. Your divine Author has already penned a masterpiece about you that He would like to share one step at a time. God is relentlessly committed and lovingly devoted to you. He wants to give you the life He always intended you to have—to make your story come true.

PEERING OVER THE EDGE

Some of my favorite childhood memories are the short vacations my family took to my aunt and uncle's cabin in southern Missouri. I would explore the surrounding woods and go on make-believe missions with my trusty, Daisy Red Ryder BB gun, like a special-ops soldier on assignment.

I would fire that amazing, air-powdered weapon thousands of times on every vacation. Everywhere I went, my imagination took me on incredible adventures.

I loved to stand on the cliffs overlooking a nearby river and shoot my BBs down into the water. There was a drought one year; the normally deep and fast-flowing river was shallow and docile. One summer day, the ground gave way as I stood about six feet from the edge of the cliff. The whole section crumpled and I tumbled down in a cloud of dirt and rocks.

Fortunately, a neighbor boy saw me fall and ran to get my parents. I was soon rescued and taken to the hospital, where I was treated for a concussion, cuts, and bruises, but no broken bones. Luckily, my BB gun also survived the fall, and we both fought valiantly after that.

However, my fanciful days of freedom were suddenly curtailed. My parents kept asking me, "Why were you so close to the cliffs? What were you thinking?" They stressed how blessed I was that I survived the fall and how I had to be more cautious. And where they once seemed carefree, they now constantly worried about me.

But that's how it is. Dangerous and tragic events teach us important lessons, whether we're kids on vacation or adults experiencing heartbreak. Experience makes us hesitate and stay away from the dangerous cliffs of life that we used to frequent. The advice of those who are no longer adventurous sidelines our own adventures. Caution kills our curiosity and we become risk-adverse. The attractions of life's dangerous places no longer hold the same allure.

BY AVOIDING THE UNKNOWN AND PLAYING IT
SAFE, YOU CAN MISS THE CHANCE
TO FIND OUT WHO YOU ARE AND WHAT YOU
ARE MEANT TO EXPERIENCE.

Sometimes in life, the greatest opportunities lie in the unknown and danger is mixed into our destiny. By avoiding the unknown and playing it safe, you can miss the chance to find out who you are and what you are meant to experience. Maybe it's time for you to peer over the cliffs again. The Holy Spirit is ready to teach us God's vision for our lives.

> *No eye has seen, no ear has heard, and no mind has imagined what God has prepared for those who love him…. No one can know God's thoughts except God's own Spirit. And we have received God's Spirit (not the world's spirit), so we can know the wonderful things God has freely given us.* (1 Corinthians 2:9, 11–12)

One of my goals for this book is to increase your curiosity and decrease your caution. I am praying that God will create a *holy wonder* in you about the future He has for you. I am praying for a dissatisfaction with the status quo of your existence and asking God to move you out of your comfort zone. Life cannot be lived fully without risk. The cliffs of your destiny are calling. The ground may seem precarious, but the view is spectacular! The good stuff—God's stuff—is always near the edge.

CREATIVE OVERKILL

> *God saw everything that he had made, and behold, it was very good.* (Genesis 1:31 ESV)

I once watered and fertilized my garden to death. I fed my future vegetables so much that I destroyed them with something that was designed to help them.

I have a habit of overdoing just about everything. I tend to overdevelop, overthink, overload every message, and overwrite every paragraph. I must self-edit or I drown my ideas with too many words. My creativity must be limited because *I* am limited.

But what is true for me is not true for God, the ultimate Creator and creative genius. His creation—the universe and everything in it—will take your breath away. But His greatest creation is *us*, a work in progress. For Him, enough is never enough until His vision for you is completely realized. "*We are God's handiwork, created in Christ Jesus to do good works*" (Ephesians 2:10 NIV).

We are His creation. This is both a basic truth and a divine revelation, particularly when you consider the magnificent complexity of the human body, the sophistication and remarkable diversity of humanity, and the unique individualism of everyone you know. These all indicate the intelligence and power of the Creator.

> *In the beginning the Word already existed. The Word was with God, and the Word was God. He existed in the beginning with God. God created everything through him, and nothing was created except through him.* (John 1:1–3)

YOU ARE PART OF THE CONTINUAL EXPRESSION OF JESUS'S CREATIVE GENIUS. AND HE'S NOT DONE YET BECAUSE *YOU* ARE NOT DONE.

Everything was created through Jesus, which means you are part of the continual expression of His creative genius. And He's not done yet because *you* are not done. Jesus is so committed to his *creative intentions* toward you that He died to redeem you.

When Adam and Eve sinned, creation rebelled against the Creator. Not wanting to be separated from His creation, the Creator took the punishment that we deserved upon Himself. Jesus died and rose again so that the life He originally intended for us could be possible again. *"He died for all, so that all those who live would no longer live for themselves, but for Him who died and was raised for their sake"* (2 Corinthians 5:15 AMP). We are His redeemed creation. How great is the love of the Creator for His creation!

DESIGNED FOR A PURPOSE

Woodworking has been a hobby of mine since childhood. When my wife, Jeanne, and I were engaged, I created a wooden jewelry box for her that she still treasures and uses to this day, thirty years later. Every time she uses it, she's reminded of how much I love her.

That jewelry box was designed with a specific purpose in mind. If, God forbid, I ever got mad at her, removed her jewelry, and put my fishing lures in there, the gift that once brought joy would now cause pain. And that jewelry box would make a lousy tackle box because it was not designed for that purpose. My creation would fail to fulfill my original intention.

In a similar way, we have been lovingly designed by God for a specific purpose. We can fill our life with lesser things, but He lovingly designed us to hold the treasure of destiny. He created us with the capacity to fulfill all He has planned for us.

NO MATTER HOW FAR YOU ARE FROM THE LIFE THAT GOD PLANNED FOR YOU, YOUR PURPOSE HAS NOT CHANGED.

No matter how far you are from the life that God planned for you, your purpose has not changed. You may have brought junk into your life, but God's original, loving intention for you is still very much alive. He would love to see you brought back to a life of His divine design. No life that you could create on your own is better than the one He intends for you.

CALLED TO HOPE

If we are ever going to embrace the truth that God has *divine intentions* for us, we must be a people of hope. Paul wrote to the church at Ephesus, *"I pray that the eyes of your heart may be enlightened in order that you may know **the hope to which he has called you**"* (Ephesians 1:18 NIV). My goal is to help you see that there are God-ordained plans for you and He wants those plans to be your reality.

Can you give yourself permission to consider the possibility of a life beyond what you're experiencing right now? A decision to believe is more than a platitude or a therapeutic exercise of self-encouragement. Embracing hope is the genesis of a whole new existence. Nothing great ever happens until someone is brave enough to hope for it in their mind, soul, and spirit.

Even creation itself hopes for a better future. Writing about the curse that sin brought to the earth, Paul wrote, *"With eager hope, the creation looks forward to the day when it will join God's children in glorious freedom from death and decay"* (Romans 8:20–21). He is saying that one day, God will redeem creation just as He has redeemed us. But note the key phrase: creation will *"**join** God's children in glorious freedom."* In other words, we are ahead of the rest of creation. We who know Christ have a hope that is more advanced than everything else. We have already been redeemed. We have already been given new life. Creation marvels at the hope we have been given.

We are called to hope. My prayer for this book is the same one that Paul prayed over the Ephesians: *"I pray that the eyes of your heart may be enlightened in order that you may know the hope to which he has called you"* (Ephesians 1:18 NIV). I pray that your mind and heart overflow with hope. And I pray you will experience everything God has intended for you.

PART I:

RESCUED

ONE

THE RESCUE

He reached down from heaven and rescued me;
he drew me out of deep waters.
—Psalm 18:16

On the coast of North Carolina stands a unique landmark to the maritime history of the United States. The Chicamacomico Life-Saving Station is a stout wooden structure that was built to survive the worst storms. The brave people who served at this outpost and others like it had a simple mission: "Rescue those who cannot save themselves."

The Chicamacomico crew performed one of the greatest water rescues of all time on August 18, 1918, during World War I. The British tanker *Mirlo* was northbound along the Atlantic coast when it was torpedoed by a German submarine. Its oil and gasoline cargo caused more explosions and the rough seas turned the *Mirlo's* debris into floating weaponry that would destroy any approaching rescue vessels. Ignoring the dangers, the daring and well-trained men of Chicamacomico forced their way into the middle of the wreckage and saved forty-two *Mirlo* crew members.

This story is a great illustration of the love of someone who is willing to *rescue* others who cannot save themselves. Jesus once said, *"Greater love has no one than this: to lay down one's life for one's friends"* (John 15:13 NIV). To risk your life to save another is an expression of love and an act of valor beyond measure.

When I am exposed to stories like this one, my tendency is to contemplate what I would have done. *How would I have performed? Would my courage have taken me out to sea to help?* But the deeper issue at play here is really my own apprehension about my need to be rescued. And I am not the only one.

Why is it that when we read about the rescue of the *Mirlo* crew and similar stories, we don't ever picture ourselves floating among the wreckage and flames? Why is it our tendency to imagine that we would be among the brave rescuers? Maybe it's because if we admit our need to be rescued, we feel vulnerable. In contrast, believing we are the rescuer makes us feel strong, even when we are not.

It's vital that we begin to place our need to be rescued above the fantasy of being a rescuer—because vulnerability is always a much better starting point for change than strength. The latter gives us reason to boast; the former encourages authenticity, honesty, and an opportunity to humble ourselves. When we embrace vulnerability, we recognize that we need help and we need to trust someone. It's not easy, but it is essential for the restorative process. We may be rescuers someday, but for now, we need to be saved. The journey to where God wants you begins with being rescued from where you are.

If the *Mirlo* crew had refused to let the Chicamacomico team save them, the fiery waters would have taken their lives. Our own self-reliance may be our greatest enemy. U.S. Coast Guard divers say that the first thing a drowning person must do when being rescued is *stop trying to save themselves.* The flailing drowning victim puts both himself and his rescuer in jeopardy. Rescue demands submission.

WE ALL NEED TO BE RESCUED

What do you need rescued from? Some people know they are drowning and being pulled into the dark waters of despair. They know the flames are out of control and they're about to lose everything. It may be easy for them to submit to being rescued.

Others think their life isn't so bad and there's no need for rescue. They think, *Sure, I'd like a better life and have a few regrets. Rescue? That's a bit of a stretch.* It's hard to humble ourselves and admit that we need help. But *rescue* is a foundational part of the life God wants you to have.

I first recognized my own need for rescue as a teen. I have the best parents in the world, but my family wasn't focused on church or salvation. By age sixteen, I was searching, depressed, and defeated. My self-worth had reached the bottom of the proverbial barrel, leaving me vulnerable to addiction. I was hooked on pornography, experimenting with alcohol and drugs, and sometimes so miserable that I was suicidal. Then a life-long friend asked me to attend a church service with him. I was so desperate for answers that I quickly accepted his invitation.

Sitting in that church, I was exposed to the Bible's teachings for the first time. I can remember the fog of self-deception lifting as I absorbed every word. I began to see my own sinfulness and my need for God. I heard about the love of Jesus and recognized my need for the salvation He was offering. Drowning in the vast ocean of my failures, I knew I could never swim to the shore on my own. I asked Jesus to *rescue* me…and He reached down, lifted me out of my mess, and saved me. My depression and turmoil were replaced with joy and peace.

Other friends accused me of using religion as a "crutch," telling me I was too weak to make it on my own. At the time, I didn't know how to respond to them—but now I do. My faith in Christ is not a crutch, but a stretcher. When I could not do anything to save myself, Jesus came to my rescue.

We begin our new life of seeking God's *divine intentions* for us by acknowledging that we are individually inadequate, desperate, and sinful, and recognizing that we don't have the ability to save ourselves. In short, we admit our need for rescue. The psalmist understood this when he wrote, *"In your righteousness, rescue me and deliver me; turn your ear to me and save me"* (Psalm 71:2 NIV). He knew he could not save himself. We all have to get to that place. We all need a savior. We all need to be rescued.

The Bible uses the analogy of "sickness" when describing our need for rescue. Hoping people would understand their desperate need for Him, Jesus said, *"Healthy people don't need a doctor—sick people do. I have come to call not those who think they are righteous, but those who know they are sinners"* (Mark 2:17).

YOU CAN POSSESS WHAT GOD DESIRES FOR
YOU ONLY WHEN YOU REALIZE THAT YOU ARE
UNWORTHY AND INCAPABLE OF EARNING IT.

People who know how sick they are will want to be rescued. To experience God's best, we must acknowledge the broken parts of our lives. Transformation begins with knowing that you need it. You can possess what God desires for you only when you realize that you are unworthy and incapable of earning it. The Bible says, *"God opposes the proud but gives grace to the humble"* (James 4:6). Humility is the key to the blessings that God has reserved for you. Say it with me: "I need to be rescued. I cannot save myself. I need a savior."

THE BARGAINING PHASE

As a pastor, I made it my focus to help people get to the place where they acknowledge their need to be rescued. Many people struggle greatly with this realization and go into what I call *bargaining* mode. They try to compromise by creating an ineffective combination of their own efforts and God's ability to rescue them. They want God's help, but not at the expense of giving up their control. They want His wisdom, but not at the expense of their logic. They want His blessings, but only if they can strike a bargain that preserves their own pride.

This bargaining phase only lengthens their struggle. Divine help always begins with human humility and admission of weakness. Paul said the Lord told him, *"My grace is all you need. My power works best in weakness"* (2 Corinthians 12:9). Denying our weakness only keeps us away from God's power. God's wisdom is found at the end of our bargaining. Miracles come to those who know they need one.

DIVINE HELP ALWAYS BEGINS WITH HUMAN HUMILITY AND ADMISSION OF WEAKNESS.

There's a lot at stake here. You and I are either living in the fullness of what our divine Creator intended for us to have…or we are not. Most of us are not. Most of are not even scratching the surface of God's divine intentions for our lives. If this reality is going to change, then we all must begin in a radical place. We must be honest with ourselves and stop trying to bargain with God. We have to stop minimizing our circumstances and overestimating our strengths.

If you're looking for minor changes in your life, this may not be the book for you. I'm not trying to cover up your flaws with a little makeup or a new haircut. I'm trying to help you go through a transformation.

Start with a simple prayer to the God who loves you: "Rescue me." This prayer is both an admission of where you are and the foundational first step of the journey to where God wants you to be.

A GOD WHO RESCUES

Even a casual student of the Scriptures knows that God is a rescuer. Paul says Jesus *"gave himself for our sins to rescue us from the present evil age"* (Galatians 1:4 NIV) Luke says Jesus came to *"proclaim liberty to the captives"* (Luke 4:18 ESV). How amazing it is that the Son of God, the Creator of the universe, would care enough to rescue us and involve Himself in human misery. He is like a loving father who would go to the ends of the earth to rescue his child. God loves us so much that He is compelled to save us from the lives we were not meant to live.

GOD LOVES US SO MUCH THAT HE IS COMPELLED TO SAVE US FROM THE LIVES WE WERE NOT MEANT TO LIVE.

In a letter to Timothy, his son in faith, Paul wrote that Jesus *"gave himself as a **ransom** for all people"* (1 Timothy 2:6 NIV). When we think of a *ransom*, we think of someone being held against their will whose captors are demanding a high price for their freedom. Their only hope is that someone will pay the ransom. We think of kidnappers in an action movie or TV show.

But in real life, our captivity is more than a concept and our need for rescue is real. This verse lays it out clearly: *"An evil man is held captive by his own sins; they are ropes that catch and hold him"* (Proverbs 5:22). Jesus tells us, *"Everyone who sins is a slave of sin"* (John 8:34). Jesus came to earth to rescue us from our *slavery* to the things of this world that corrupt and control us. He pays the ransom that we could never pay on our own.

When the slaves were freed after the Civil War, many of them became sharecroppers and lived little better than they had previously. They were rescued from slavery, yes, but they had next to nothing. God never rescues like that. After liberating us from a life of bondage and oppression, He offers us true freedom and abundant life. Jesus proclaimed, *"If the Son sets you free, you will be free indeed"* (John 8:36 NIV). The word *indeed* here means something *undeniable* and *without question*. Our God rescues us *for* something, not just *from* something.

The real question for all of us is, "What is my *something*? What is God rescuing me for?" Our something may be bigger than we can imagine, but we can reduce it to one word: *calling*. When God rescues us from an inferior life, He wants to lead us toward the superior life we were meant to live, a life driven by our calling.

My life's *calling* has included ministry, family, friendships, and multiple providential assignments from God. I have lived a richer life than I would have had if I followed my own plans. My intentions pale in comparison to what God intended for me. My plans for me were local; God's plans for me were international. My plans were mostly selfish; God's plans for me were selfless. My plans coddled my fears; God's plans made me face all my fears and overcome them with His help. My plans were simple; God's plans have been profound, productive, and extensive.

Your *calling* is not your profession—it's the life you were meant to live. God rescues you so you can become the person He has called you to be, then He empowers you so you can accomplish that calling. Rescue is where your calling begins.

RARE RESCUES WE ALL NEED

Everyone needs to be saved from *something*. We all encounter people or circumstances that strive to steal our freedom, but these are not our greatest foes.

Let me point out three *rare rescues* that everyone needs. These liberation forces will clear the pathway to your future and allow you to pursue the life God designed for you.

RESCUED FROM OURSELVES

When we think of the word *rescue*, we usually think of a hostage being liberated, someone saved from a burning building, or similar scenarios. But we often need to be *rescued from ourselves*. Our greatest enemies are internal and elusive; they have more power to harm us than anyone else. Our endless fears. Our sinful desires. Our unruly thoughts. The voices in our heads rattle like a guard's keys as he walks past the prison cells. We are trapped within, not sure what the issues are or how we can get out. We stand in the way of our own freedom.

What we need to be rescued from goes beyond destructive *behaviors*. Lurking in the shadows, whispering to us and leading us toward self-destruction, is what theologians call our *sin nature* or *earthy nature*. Even the apostle Paul admitted he could not conquer his sinful nature without divine intervention. (See Romans 7:21–25.)

OUR GREATEST ENEMIES ARE INTERNAL AND ELUSIVE; THEY HAVE MORE POWER TO HARM US THAN ANYONE ELSE.

Charles Spurgeon once said, "As the salt flavors every drop in the Atlantic, so does sin affect every atom of our nature. It is so sadly there, so abundantly there, that if you cannot detect it, you are deceived." Sin infects us all. After committing adultery with Bathsheba, King David declared, *"I was born a sinner—yes, from the moment my mother conceived me"* (Psalm 51:5). The battles you and I are facing have been with us since birth. The thief stealing the life you want to live is *you*. It's all an inside job.

Ever wonder why your bad habits and evil desires follow you from place to place? Even changing the environment you live in fails to produce lasting behavioral results. When we deal with the external without addressing the internal, we are left with frustration. Why? Because you have not dealt with hidden issues of your own nature. No matter how well you are nurtured, the inward pull of an unruly nature is always there. Its force is constant and dominant. It is like a sinful form of gravity that slowly but surely forces you back to a sobering reality: "You can't do this on your own because *you* are a big part of the problem." When your *nature* is in charge, there will always be *natural disasters*. Like a tornado in the Midwest or a hurricane along the East Coast, your nature will strike without warning and work against the life you are trying to build.

The answer is to seek help outside yourself. Paul told the Romans, *"Letting your sinful nature control your mind leads to death. But letting the Spirit control your mind leads to life and peace"* (Romans 8:6). When our sinful natures are submitted to the life-changing power of the Spirit of God, death gives way to life. Tranquility replaces chaos. When the internal war is won, you are free to build the life God desires for you.

How do you battle the enemy inside you? You begin with an *invitation* to the Spirit of God. Jesus conquered sin and death on the cross; He has the power to save you from yourself by forgiving your sins and placing His Holy Spirit inside you. Your life will then be empowered by the Spirit and not dominated by your sinful nature. God will transform your life by changing you from the inside out.

In dealing with this issue, Paul tells us, *"Those who are still under the control of their sinful nature can never please God. But you are not controlled by your sinful nature...if you have the Spirit of God living in you"* (Romans 8:8–9).

AS LONG AS *YOU* ARE CONTROLLING YOU, YOU WILL NEVER BE ABLE TO PLEASE GOD BECAUSE YOU CANNOT PLEASE HIM WITHOUT HIS HELP.

As long as *you* are controlling you, you will never be able to please God because you cannot please Him without His help. But when you *invite* Jesus to live in you, the Holy Spirit enters in and takes control. Now you can have the life that God intends for you to have because you are no longer sabotaging yourself. As you learn to submit to the control of the Spirit of God living inside you, a world of endless possibilities opens. You can finally live the life you're supposed to enjoy.

I remember inviting Jesus to come into my heart to rescue me from my sins. I was trapped within myself; I could never win a war where the enemy had full access to all of me. So I invited the Warrior of all warriors, the King of all kings, to take over and win the war within me. That day, my internal battles were dealt a death blow. I admit, I still experience a few skirmishes, struggles, and squabbles. But with the Spirit of God living inside me, the war for my future has already been won.

ASK JESUS TO COME INTO YOUR HEART

Why not invite Jesus to come into your heart right now? Pray this prayer with me:

> Jesus, come into my heart and take control. Forgive me for my sins and overcome my sinful nature. Conquer the enemy within me by the power of Your Spirit. Thank You for nailing my sin to the cross and for defeating death itself by way of Your resurrection. I give You the life I have because I want the life You have for me. I give up my human aspirations because I want Your divine intentions. In Your name I pray, amen.

When you pray this kind of invitation to God, you open yourself up to all that He has formulated for you. Your *ship* now has a captain and, thankfully, it's no longer you! With God on the *inside*, you can begin to change the *outside*. The transformation of your *soul* will be the catalyst for the transformation of your *life*. The key is to live from Spirit power rather than willpower. His power changes everything because His power changes you.

Paul encapsulates this truth when He writes:

> *The Spirit of God, who raised Jesus from the dead, lives in you. And just as God raised Christ Jesus from the dead, he will give life to your mortal bodies by this same Spirit living within you. **Therefore**, dear brothers and sisters, you have no obligation to do what your sinful nature urges you to do. For if you live by its dictates, you will die. But if through the power of the Spirit you put to death the deeds of your sinful nature, you will live. For all who are led by the Spirit of God are children of God.* (Romans 8:11–14)

I love the *therefore* of verse 12. The Spirit of God lives in us, *therefore* we are not obligated to sin. There is someone new in charge. We can *live* because our sinful nature has been *put to death*. Internal change leads to external possibilities. Your rescued soul sets the stage for your redeemed life.

RESCUED FROM OUR PLANS

When I was little, my dreams were ever evolving. I started out wanting to be a *trash man*! I remember watching them through the front window of our house and thinking, "They have it all!" These guys get to ride on big trucks, hang out with their buddies, and crush things. As an added bonus, they get their pick of free stuff that people leave out on the curb! How cool is that?

My dreams evolved as I got older. At various times, I wanted to be a professional fisherman, a fireman, a carpenter, and a police officer. That last one stuck with me. At age sixteen, I was convinced that I would one day graduate from the police academy and become an officer. I had some noble dreams, but none of them were what God planned for me. In His infinite wisdom, God called me into the ministry. He called me to speak and eventually to write for His glory.

I have had thousands of opportunities to tell others about the great love of Jesus. I have lived a life that is beyond what I could ever have imagined. I had my *plans*, but God had His *purpose*. I knew what I wanted, but what I wanted was not what God intended. I am grateful every day that my life has resulted in a fulfillment of His destiny instead of my desire. I thank God that He rescued me from my plans.

King Solomon, the wisest man who ever lived, wrote: *"Many are the plans in a person's heart, but it is the LORD's purpose that prevails"* (Proverbs 19:21 NIV).

I love to make plans. Nothing gets me more excited about the future. *Where are we going to go? What will we do? What will it all look like? How will we accomplish it all?* To me, these questions are as fun as they are practical. Planning is a good and necessary thing. But we must remember that our *plans* and God's *purpose* are not always the same thing. In fact, unless your life is fully submitted to God, your plans are probably getting in the way of God's purpose.

WE MUST REMEMBER THAT OUR *PLANS* AND GOD'S *PURPOSE* ARE NOT ALWAYS THE SAME THING.

Here is one example: when I plan something, I always plan to succeed. If I am starting a new business or ministry, I plan to succeed at every level, telling myself, *The opening will be a grand one and the first year's profits will break records. The church will explode with growth and the people will give generously.* My plans never include struggle and they certainly don't include failure. They leave *little* room for character development, but *lots* of room for personal advancement. My plans are always problematic because they rarely factor in the deeper aspects of God's purposes. But God loves me—and you!—far too much to let us plan without the guidance of His great purpose. His purpose *prevails* over our plans. This in itself is a form of *rescue.*

In Proverbs 19:21, King Solomon wrote that we have many plans in our *heart.* That sounds like a good thing, right? After all, society encourages us to "follow our hearts" and "live from the heart." Sailing through life with your heart as your captain means you will live the life you're supposed to live...right?

But the heart *is* the problem. The center of our emotional being, it's driven by emotions. The heart is a wonderful thing, but it isn't a trustworthy guide. Your biggest choices in life require you to act without depending on your emotions. Our own plans cannot be fully trusted because they come from the heart.

The prophet Jeremiah said, "*The heart is deceitful above all things, and desperately wicked; who can know it?*" (Jeremiah 17:9 NKJV). You probably have heard the phrase "the heart wants what it wants." What if what your heart wants does not coincide with what God wants? What if your heart is trying to deceive you into a life you were not meant to live? We should follow God and question our hearts.

Sometimes, I have to be rescued from my own escape plan. I am easily deceived by my own desires. What I think is my path to happiness and fulfillment must be cautiously tested and carefully evaluated. I must consistently arrive at a place of spiritual neutrality. This is where I position myself to only want what God wants. I consciously take my foot off my mind's gas and brake pedals and remove my hands from the steering wheel. I want God to drive my thoughts so I can end up where He wants me to be. I discipline myself to live with an attitude that submits to His will and trusts His intentions. We must all arrive at a place such as this, a place of neutrality where things are not predetermined and God is truly in charge of our lives.

RESCUED FOR A REASON

My father used to work for a levee district in charge of some levees bordering the Mississippi River. He often worked at one of the pump stations controlling the river when it's at flood stage. During one major flood, my father witnessed an unfortunate man who was too close to the water and got swept into the raging current. The man helplessly struggled to save himself and was begging for someone to rescue him. Dad wanted to help, but jumping in would have been a death sentence for both of them. Rescuing the man was beyond his capabilities.

Now, in my mind, my father is bigger than life and can do anything. He would risk his safety in a heartbeat to help anyone who was in need. But even my dad could not help that drowning man. The truth is, all earthly fathers are limited. No one is as strong as they would like to be; everyone is inadequate. A person's ability to *rescue* another is wrapped in a package of frustrating limitations. Superheroes exist only in the movies. There are times when we may be able to save someone who's drowning, but at other times, all we can do is watch.

We certainly cannot save someone's soul or give them a purpose for living. Only God can do that.

Maybe you have been caught in the *current* of a life that is taking you away from where you want to be. This world will offer you lots of solutions. Just stay up late tonight and flip around the channels on your TV. You will soon find infomercials that will give you easy steps toward a new and better you. For only three payments of $19.95, plus shipping and handling, you can order up a miracle cure.

A PERSON'S ABILITY TO *RESCUE* ANOTHER IS WRAPPED IN A PACKAGE OF FRUSTRATING LIMITATIONS. SUPERHEROES EXIST ONLY IN THE MOVIES.

But in your sprit, in the deepest part of your being, you will sense the false hope. Sometimes, it seems like the whole world is standing on the riverbanks of our lives, offering us everything but a real rescue. No one is jumping in the waters to save us. Which makes sense—because they are drowning, too. What we need is one who is greater than what is consuming us. What we need is Jesus.

When you are being swept away and are about to go under, cry out to Him for rescue. Forget the natural and turn to the supernatural. The Bible says, *"If you need wisdom, ask our generous God, and he will give it to you. He will not rebuke you for asking"* (James 1:5). Do you know how to overcome the present and navigate the future? Neither do I. But God does! Ask your *"generous God"* and He will give you the wisdom you need. Jesus is full of wisdom. (See Mark 6:2.) Your Savior has solutions to your problems and a direction for your future—and His plans are strategic and infinite. You want to know what He knows because His wisdom is your lifeline and He is your rescuer.

A drowning person does not check his calendar for future appointments. When you're fighting for your life, planning your future is a low priority. About all the *planning* you can handle is keeping your head above water and praying for rescue. But with rescue comes an explosion of ambition. Suddenly, a newly saved person wants to accomplish all of the things they have left undone. They want to see places they have never seen. They want to be the person they have failed to be. Getting rescued from the jaws of death activates vision. Nothing makes someone want to live like almost dying.

I have a picture in my spirit of Jesus on the riverbank your life. He dove in and pulled you out of the depths of despair. He breathes life into your lungs and He makes your heart beat again. Then, as He is drying you off, He begins to speak to you about your future. Only moments ago, He rescued you and He is already revealing the plans that He has for you. He is so eager for you to know all of the things He has in store for you. You almost died, so now, He wants to show you how to live. He wants you to know that you were rescued for a reason.

> For we are God's masterpiece. He has created us anew in Christ Jesus, so we can do the good things he planned for us long ago.
>
> (Ephesians 2:10)

This verse assures us that God planned *"good things"* for us *"long ago."* Jesus is eager to rescue you so He can show you the blueprints He has for your life. He has been holding on to these plans for you for a long time. He wants to pull you out of your mess so He can show them to you. What are God's plans for you? That is a journey for *you* to discover and I hope this book helps you with that breakthrough. I only know His plans are *good*, even if we've messed up terribly.

One of the best examples of a people drowning in a sea of bad choices comes from the book of Jeremiah. For generations, Israel had lived outside of God's best. Now, they were held captive by a foreign power, with little hope for rescue. In the middle of this hopelessness, God starts talking about His *plans* and a new life for His people. The prophet gives them God's message:

> *"For I know the plans I have for you," declares the* Lord, *"plans to prosper you and not to harm you, plans to give you hope and a future."*
>
> (Jeremiah 29:11 NIV)

God goes beyond their need to be rescued and talks about His intended future for them. He lets them know that His plans will make them prosperous and hopeful. His plans did not end at Israel being rescued; they began there. It was a future they never conceived, a future He intended for them.

Like the people of ancient Israel, *you* have been rescued for an unimaginable reason. God's reason.

DISCOVERY QUESTIONS

Why is it hard to think that you might need to be rescued?

_____

_____

_____

_____

What bargains have you tried to make with God?

_____

_____

_____

_____

Why can the heart lead you to do something you regret?

_____

_____

_____

_____

How does knowing that God has _divine intentions_ for you affect your outlook on life?

_____

_____

_____

_____

TWO

FAITH TO SEE

*We live by **faith**, not by **sight**.*
—2 Corinthians 5:7 (NIV)

L et's play the "what if" game. Let's imagine that your personal history is far different than what actually happened. Although it may be difficult, I want you to fantasize that your *past* was nothing short of *perfection*. Like many people, you may have grown up in a home where your family fought and had harsh words for one another. Maybe you were poor. Maybe you felt misunderstood for one reason or another.

Now imagine something radically different. Picture yourself growing up in a *perfect*, loving home, a place of peace where you heard words of love, healing, and mutual respect. Your environment was filled with encouragement and serenity. Try to place yourself in the middle of this new, imaginary place. Would your new past change anything? Would it change you?

Let's take this a step further. Perhaps you have developed destructive habits that robbed you of the life you were meant to experience. Think back to where the addictions began—that first joint, that first lustful look at pornography, that first violent video game, or even that first innocent bite of cheesecake. Now, abandon that memory and recall a new one, a better one. See yourself as disciplined and pure. Imagine yourself with a great metabolism, a desire for wholesome foods, and a natural love for exercise and the great outdoors, all of which have made you the picture of vitality and well-being.

Now we're getting somewhere, so let's keep going.

Envision a pristine past where you never experienced hurt, anger, abuse, or abandonment. Everyone in this fantasy world encouraged you. You never developed bad habits and you were surrounded by everything you needed to thrive and grow. Any negativity and pain in your real life never existed. To make this story more realistic, we will give you a few minor struggles for character development, but nothing you can't handle, nothing that causes you to take a detour into a dark pit of personal destruction.

What would your life would be like right now if your past resembled the fictitious tale we just created? What if you grew up with everything you needed for the development of a productive life? Who would you be today if you were only exposed to perfection, if you had never been hurt? Imagine all of these narratives for a minute or two. Take your time....

IMAGINE YOU HAVE NEVER SINNED...

Now, let's dream even bigger. Imagine that you are morally pure and spiritually strong and you always have been this way. You have never sinned; you have always obeyed God, loved God, and never strayed from Him. In fact, you have always been surrounded by people who were also without sin—saints, just like you. You've never had addictive tendencies and you live with complete freedom and selfless love.

How would this impact your life? What kind of a person do you think you would be if your past was sinless and perfect?

First, you would naturally be more like Jesus. You would be fearless and filled with joy. You would possess fully developed gifts and your life would be filled with purpose. You would not be plagued by insecurities because you never wandered into places where insecurities breed. You would be loving and giving and you would enjoy relationships that are important and meaningful. Your appealing personality would be on full display to those around you. Life would be wonderful because you are the person you were meant to be. You always embraced God's plans for your life, so there would be no deviation, no disappointment, and no disaster. Every aspect of your destiny would be fulfilled. You would be so happy because you were living the life and being the person you were always meant to be. Imagine that!

Poof! Game over. This may be a fun exercise, maybe even a therapeutic one, but it has little value because of one big problem: *you.* Even if we could magically trade our real pasts for imaginary ones, we probably would still self-sabotage our dream scenarios and clutter our lives with destructive behavior. Your imperfect nature would override your perfect nurturing. All of our *natures* are bent toward self-destruction. Even if you could change the *nurture* part of your past, how would you deal with your sinful *nature?*

Unfortunately, our imaginary scenario is the ultimate in pure fantasy. Life is not like that and never could be. Paul deals with this very issue in his letter to the Romans: *"All have sinned and fall short of the glory of God"* (Romans 3:23 NKJV). You have sinned—and so have I. Our pasts are far from perfect.

GOD SEES YOU WHOLE AND RESTORED,
A VERSION OF YOU THAT'S BEYOND
YOUR COMPREHENSION.

I took you on this imaginary journey because I want you to have a miniscule glimpse of the person God imagines you to be. I want you to see yourself as whole, the way God sees you. God sees you in His perfection. He sees past your brokenness because He knows what a restored version of you would look like. All that was done *to* you or *by* you is not enough to stop His vision of you. God sees you in a way that you cannot possibly see yourself. He sees you whole and restored, a version of you that's beyond your comprehension. This is why you have to lean on God's perception of the person you are meant to be. He knows the life you're supposed to be living, the life your painful history stole from you. A better past will always be the work of fantasy...but a better future is a dream that can come true.

KNOW WHAT HE KNOWS

I live in Missouri, "the Show-Me State." I was not consulted about this slogan because I was not alive when they made it up. Had I been asked, I would not have voted for it. It doesn't resonate with me because it reflects a lack of imagination. Demanding proof up front is the best way to stop imagination in its tracks. It's also the best way to kill faith. Even so, it's an inherent part of our human nature to want to see something before we accept it. This is why faith is so difficult. We want to *see* before we *believe*, but the Bible shows us that we must *believe* before we can *see*.

God honors *faith* and faith always positions believing before seeing. God loves it when we combine imagination with faith. *Faith* and *imagination* are inseparable forces. You cannot possess one without the other. This imagination/faith combo enables us to believe Him before we experience the focus of our faith. Faith is ultimately a God-given ability to imagine something different, something better. Anyone can believe what is right before their eyes. It doesn't require faith or imagination.

The writer of the letter to the Hebrews had a faith-filled imagination when he defined faith for us. In a moment of divine inspiration, he wrote, *"Now faith is the substance of things **hoped for**, the evidence of things **not seen**"* (Hebrews 11:1 NKJV).

FAITH ASKS US TO PLACE OUR
SPIRIT-INSPIRED IMAGINATIONS ABOVE AND
BEYOND WHAT WE CAN SEE.

Faith *hopes* (imagines better) and sees what cannot be seen. By definition, faith is imaginative. Faith asks us to place our spirit-inspired imaginations above and beyond what we can see. We might not think to use words like *substance* or *evidence* to conclusively and convincingly explain faith, but these are the terms the writer to the Hebrews used.

Our *faith* is supposed to be a weighty thing, something of substance. It should be strong enough that it provides evidence of our belief and proves the validity of what God says about us. No matter what our eyes are telling us, we choose to believe what God has said.

There's just one requirement if you wish to discover God's divine intentions for you and the life He desires for you: you must *choose* to have faith. If you cannot, by faith, imagine *you* as the person God has envisioned, then this book will be of little value to you. If you cannot *see it*, you will not have the courage to *be it*. The writer to the Hebrews said, *"It is impossible to please God without faith"* (Hebrews 11:6). God demands our faith. It brings pleasure to Him. If by faith, you choose to imagine and believe what God has said about you, there is no limit to the transformation that will take place in your life.

IF BY FAITH, YOU CHOOSE TO IMAGINE AND
BELIEVE WHAT GOD HAS SAID ABOUT YOU, THERE
IS NO LIMIT TO THE TRANSFORMATION THAT WILL
TAKE PLACE IN YOUR LIFE.

Don't you wonder, *What has God imagined about me?* It's humbling to think that the Creator of the universe has imagined anything about *us* as individuals—and yet He has. I think this is what David was feeling when he wrote, *"How precious are your thoughts about me, O God. They cannot be numbered! I can't even count them; they outnumber the grains of sand"* (Psalm 139:17–18).

Our God—infinitely knowledgeable, creative, loving, powerful, and forgiving—has precious thoughts about *you*. His thoughts about you are so vast, they *"cannot be numbered!"* God is thoughtfully obsessed with you!

I wonder what God finds so interesting about you and me? I just don't get it. I'm not interesting enough for anyone to have innumerable thoughts about me! But according to God, I am *that* intriguing—and so are *you*. His thoughts concerning us are *priceless* because they are divine. You are on His mind all the time and I pray that you will become highly curious about what God is imagining about you.

God wants you to know what He is thinking. He wants to connect you to His thoughts through His Holy Spirit. Maybe Paul was contemplating this when he wrote these words to the church at Corinth:

> As it is written, "What no eye has seen, what no ear has heard, and what no human mind has conceived"—the things God has prepared for those who love him—these are the things God has revealed to us by his Spirit. The Spirit searches all things, even the deep things of God.
>
> (1 Corinthians 2:9–10 NIV)

You cannot possibly comprehend all that God is tenderly conceiving for you, but you can get a glimpse. Showing you what God thinks is a work of His Holy Spirit, who *"searches all things."* The very next verse, 2 Corinthians 2:11, tells us that the Holy Spirit fully knows God's thoughts and our thoughts. The Spirit of God is always present in the realm of our imaginations. Since it is His job to help connect us with God, the Holy Spirit is the one who reveals to us what God is thinking. He is the one who gives us imaginative faith. Right now, at this very moment, the Holy Spirit wants to bond your thoughts with the thoughts of the God who loves you. What is God thinking? We can know His thoughts if we will allow the Holy Spirit to be at work in us.

*"We are God's **masterpiece**. He has created us anew in Christ Jesus, so we can do the good things he planned for us long ago"* (Ephesians 2:10). I love

what Paul wrote in this letter so much that I made it the theme of this book.

SINCE IT IS HIS JOB TO HELP CONNECT US WITH GOD, THE HOLY SPIRIT IS THE ONE WHO REVEALS TO US WHAT GOD IS THINKING. HE GIVES US IMAGINATIVE FAITH.

A *masterpiece* is an outstanding work of art that originates in the artist's imagination. The artist has the foresight to see what no one else can see and the capability to transform raw materials into something beautiful and complex. The masterpiece God intends for you to be first existed in His imagination. His Divine mind has envisioned a version of you and your life that only He can see, which will come in His perfect timing. God takes the raw material of your existence and molds it into something masterful. Before you were born, the person you were meant to be was in His thoughts.

THE LOVE FOR JESUS IS FEARLESS

I've been blessed by a great deal of love in my life. My first love was a girl in the first grade, who I kissed behind a large trash bin. My young heart fell in love a few times after that, but I was always too scared to do anything about it. As I grew older and finally made it to high school, my capacity to love expanded. No one can love as deeply as a sixteen-year-old kid with the keys to his parents' car! I experienced love throughout my college years and finally married the love of my life. I have known the love of an amazing wife and family, incredible parents, and loyal friends.

But I never experienced a powerful, transforming love until I met Jesus. My Savior loved me like no one else ever could and His love delivered me from fear.

Jesus has that same love for *you*.

Jesus's love gives us the courage to *imagine* a better life. Before I met Jesus, I was too afraid to imagine anything extraordinary concerning me or my future. My fear was like a blinding fog that kept me from seeing more than a few inches in front of me, holding me back and preventing me from seeing the future He intended for me. But when I accepted the transforming love of Jesus into my life, His love took away my fear. Suddenly, I had the courage to dream and my imagination was freed from its restraints. The love of God lifted the fog and brought dazzling sunshine.

John, the apostle of love, amplifies this truth: *"There is no fear in love. But perfect love drives out fear"* (1 John 4:18 NIV). Jesus loves us so perfectly that if we open our hearts to Him, there is no room for fear to exist. No one else can love you like that. *Fearless* love can only be produced by God because God is the only one who has no fear or insecurities. His love invites us into His fearless world of limitless possibilities that do not exist in any other relationship.

GOD'S LOVE INVITES US INTO HIS FEARLESS WORLD OF LIMITLESS POSSIBILITIES.

The *love of Jesus* opens the door for us to become children of God. This love drives the Creator to adopt His creation. Paul described this beautiful reality when he wrote:

> *You have not received a spirit that makes you fearful slaves. Instead, you received God's Spirit when he adopted you as his own children. Now we call him, "Abba, Father." For his Spirit joins with our spirit to affirm that we are God's children. And since we are his children, **we are his heirs**. In fact, together with Christ we are heirs of God's glory.*
> (Romans 8:15–17)

Our divine adoption is deeper than what we can fully understand with human logic. More than a legal transaction, it's a spiritual reality. The Spirit affirms it and makes it so. We are His. Discovering what that means is the greatest pursuit anyone can ever have.

Paul said we are not just children of God—we are also His very heirs. God loves you so perfectly and has adopted you so completely that you are going to share in the very rewards of Jesus Himself. You get to share in *God's glory.* And nothing brings God more glory than living the life that He intended for you to have. Your story has a divine context because you are His child. You do nothing on your own because you have been adopted by Him. His power and resources are available to you. Your adoption has set you up for the future He has envisioned for you.

SOMEONE HAD FAITH TO SEE

I love the TV show *Shark Tank*.[1] It highlights aspiring entrepreneurs who make business presentations to a panel of five investors ("sharks") in the hopes that someone will invest in them. Typically, the entrepreneurs have thought of a solution to a problem or invented a product or service that could have dramatic potential. They imagined something new and decided to do something about it. For example, Arthur L. Fry wanted to be able to post little pieces of paper on his hymnal without harming it. Today, the Post-it Notes he invented are used all over the world.[2] I just bought a leaf *blower* that doubles as a leaf *vacuum*, so I can blow the leaves into a pile and then vacuum them up without ever bending over. Ingenious! Its inventor must surely be a millionaire by now.

Every time we see someone getting rich from some invention, we say, "Why didn't I think of that?" Every great accomplishment begins with someone who has envisioned something that would make a difference in people's lives. *Someone saw that.* Someone had imagination that was bigger than the problem they faced. Someone had *faith to see.*

What do you see when you look over the landscape of your life? Do you see limitations, or do you see opportunities? Innovation never thrives

1. *Shark Tank.* Created by Mark Burnett. ABC, 2009–present.
2. www.msthalloffame.org/arthur_l_fry.htm

in an environment of abundance. It's only when the drought comes, the industry dries up, the dynamics shift, and the old solutions stop working that the innovators emerge. When you must look harder, creativity has time to develop. When your path is not obvious and your solutions are not easy, it's time to press in, not give in. It's time to look harder so you might see what no one else can. There is more to your life than what meets the human eye. God wants you to see what He sees.

WHEN YOUR PATH IS NOT OBVIOUS AND YOUR SOLUTIONS ARE NOT EASY, IT'S TIME TO PRESS IN, NOT GIVE IN.

Maybe you are enveloped by personal limitations. Perhaps you are walled in by your past and can't see a way out. The good news is, faith can see through walls. The Bible says we are to *"live by faith, not by sight"* (2 Corinthians 5:7 NIV). My big, faith-filled plea in this book is that you allow yourself to see by faith. As you read through these pages, let me be your *eyes* for a little while. Sometimes, it takes someone who is not behind your *walls* to help you see a way out. Let the Holy Spirit use what you are reading to guide you through the darkness. There is light coming. You are not alone. We are on this journey together.

DISCOVERY QUESTIONS

What would a restored version of you look like?

_____

_____

_____

_____

_____

What is your *faith* causing you to *hope* for?

_____

_____

_____

_____

_____

How does knowing that God is thoughtfully obsessed with you make you feel?

_____

_____

_____

_____

_____

How does the perfect love of Jesus help you overcome your fears?

_____

_____

_____

_____

_____

THREE

DISCOVERING HOME

God makes a home for the lonely.
—Psalm 68:6 (AMP)

Those of us who grew up before everyone had cell phones remember something called a phone cord. It's hard to believe, but most of our homes only had one phone and that phone was attached to a cord. At our house, our phone hung on the wall in our dining room, next to our living room. It only had a three-foot cord, so when someone called us, we were leashed to the phone like a prisoner on a chain. This was a bad setup for private calls of any kind—especially the kind a teenage guy wants to have with the girl he loves.

It is 1984; I am sixteen and head over heels crazy in love with my high school girlfriend. We had only been dating for about six months, but she was my whole world.

One evening, the phone rang. I was sitting a few feet away in the living room with my parents, my sister, my brother, and my grandparents. Mom answered the phone and everyone giggled when she announced that my girlfriend was calling. I placed the receiver to my ear and stretched the cord as far into the dining room as I could. The love of my life sounded serious. She got right to the point, wasting no time breaking my heart by swiftly and methodically ending our relationship—over the phone! Within minutes, my world crashed in as what I cared about the most was destroyed. To make matters worse, my family had a front row seat because I was leashed to the phone cord!

I desperately pleaded with the girl. Eventually, I stopped whispering as I threw myself into the task of trying to revive our already-dead relationship. I cried. It was not my best moment. To make matters worse, Mom turned off the television so everyone could focus on me! Apparently, I was more entertaining than whatever show was on. Humiliated is not a strong enough word to describe how I felt. The drama went on for several minutes and then my now ex-girlfriend hung up on me.

DAD TRIED TO STOP ME

I was emotionally shredded. I instinctively grabbed my car keys and started for the door. I was going to drive over to her house and work everything out. Without warning, Dad suddenly stepped in front of me. He wisely told me that I was making a mistake. He was not going to let me drive while I was in this emotional state—and he took the keys from me. I then made a dangerous move, one I never would have tried if I wasn't hurting so badly. I actually shoved my dad, pushing him out of the way! Before anyone could stop me, I rushed out the front door.

My now former girlfriend lived five miles away, but I was determined. *I'm going to fix this!* I told myself. About a block from my home, I decided to cut through a graveyard. I climbed the five-foot chain-link fence that surrounded it and started to jog toward the girl's house. Then I heard some clanking behind me. I looked back…and there was my dad, struggling to get over the fence. I was sixteen and skinny; Dad was twenty-seven years older and a little overweight. But he gamely made it over the fence and started toward me.

Pridefully, I thought to myself, *You will never catch me.* I adjusted my easy jog to a medium trot and decided I would deal with the consequences later. I then glanced back to see how my dad was doing. To my surprise, he was making up ground, running at full speed. He was so much faster than I could have imagined! I thought, *You will never keep up this pace!* I turned on the jets and started running in earnest.

But then I made one last mistake. I looked back a third time and saw that Dad was losing energy fast. I could see the determination on his face; he was giving it all he had…but it was not going to be enough. I could have easily outrun him, but that didn't matter anymore. His desperation and concern overwhelmed me.

I stopped, leaned up against a tree, and waited for my father. It didn't take long for him to reach me and when he did, he didn't yell or say a single word. There was wisdom in his silence. Dad looked at me, paused for a moment, and then silently put his arm around me and walked me back home.

GOD CHASES AFTER US

My father's determination to save me from myself that day is one of my most cherished memories from my teenage years. That chase helped to shape me emotionally. It is also a living illustration of what God has done for me spiritually. Like my dad, our heavenly Father is always trying to walk us back home. We may be hurt and humiliated, we may think we can run out and fix our lives, but what we really need to do is go back home.

Pain, disappointment, and failure can make us run, but God will chase us with His love. He comes after us and we cannot outrun God's love, nor should we try. He never judges us when we stop running. Instead, He wraps His arms around us and walks us back to the place of healing. He shows us who we are and who we can be. He takes us back home.

GOD NEVER JUDGES US WHEN WE STOP
RUNNING. INSTEAD, HE WRAPS HIS ARMS
AROUND US AND WALKS US BACK TO THE PLACE
OF HEALING.

When I speak to an audience and share the story of my dad walking me home, I always pause and address a couple of elephants in the room—one named *father* and the other named *home*. Some have no concept of a loving father because they never had one. Still others cannot imagine what a safe, loving home feels like. So when I tell this story about a loving father who walks his hurting son back home, some struggle to identify with it.

This may be why the Bible repeatedly provides us with both the concept of God as our loving Father and the imagery of Him giving us a *home*. God wants to heal our perspective and redeem our broken concepts of *father* and *home*. He is the perfect representation of a good, loving Father who is everything a son or daughter would ever need. He is everything a Father is supposed to be. To find Him is to find your real home.

THE LOST SON WHO COMES HOME

Among the great biblical narratives illustrating the spiritual realities of *home* and *father* is the parable of the prodigal son found in Luke 15. In this chapter, Luke writes about three stories that Jesus shared with a crowd during His ministry—the parables of the lost sheep, the lost coin, and the lost son. The point of each story is that God will go to great lengths to search for and find the precious things that are lost. God wants all that belongs to Him to be safely at home with Him.

Jesus loved to teach using parables—concise, instructive stories that engage our imaginations and reveal spiritual truths. In the parable of the prodigal son, Jesus magnifies the great love that our heavenly Father has for His children. (See Luke 15:11–32.) Some theologians think this story should be called the parable of the loving father.

Before this, Jesus tells two short parables: one about a man who has a hundred sheep, one of which goes missing; the other about a widow who has ten silver coins and loses one. When the lost sheep and the lost coin are found, there is great rejoicing. In the same way, Jesus says, there is great joy in heaven when just one sinner repents. (See Luke 15:4–10.)

To drive home His message, Jesus tells the crowd about a wealthy man with two sons who live at home with him. The youngest son asks his father for his inheritance. Basically, he's saying he can't wait for his father to die to get his money. Surprisingly, this father—who represents our heavenly Father—simply gives up to half of his wealth to the young, rebellious son, with no arguments, no speeches, no resistance, and, apparently, no discussion. Just like our heavenly Father, this man honors the free will of his son.

Of course, in his immaturity, the son squanders the money, spending it on parties and prostitutes, and eventually finds himself in shame-filled poverty. Soon, this broken son starts thinking about *home*. He wasted his father's resources and brought dishonor to the family name. Feeling homesick, he comes up with a plan: *"I will go home to my father and say, 'Father, I have sinned against both heaven and you, and I am no longer worthy of being called your son. Please take me on as a hired servant'"* (Luke 15:18–19). Then he starts the lonely walk back home, not sure what kind of reception he will receive. He probably wonders, *What has my father been doing? Will he be disgusted and angry with me? Does he still love me?*

He doesn't realize that his father has been waiting, watching, and hoping for his return—*just as our heavenly Father waits, watches, and hopes for our return to Him!*

Jesus then puts the heart of the Father on full display: *"While he was still a long way off, his father saw him coming. Filled with love and compassion, he ran to his son, embraced him, and kissed him"* (Luke 15:20).

This father is far-sighted, just like our heavenly Father. No matter how far we are from God, He sees us and is filled with compassion. In Jesus's parable, the father has been waiting and watching, but now, with his beloved son in sight, he starts to run. The nobleman goes against protocol and propriety by spontaneously sprinting toward his son.

After the hugging and crying subside, the father first puts a clean, royal robe around his son, covering his dirty, sinful condition from working in a pig pen. He wants his son to walk home enveloped in his love. He then puts a ring on his son's finger. Many theologians believe this was a signet ring that probably carried the family crest and could be used to sign documents or purchase goods. The son had wasted half of the father's money and hurt his reputation, but that does not quench the aroma of grace filling the air. Still standing in the field a few hundred yards from the father's house, he is given access to his father's authority and resources.

The father also places sandals on his son's dirty feet. This event is filled with staggering significance. Most servants did not have sandals, so this meant the son was not going to bunk with the workers—he was going *home*. Finally, the father orders the fattened calf to be killed and cooked for a celebration feast as he leads this wayward son back to the place he never should have left.

I am sure this story stunned the Pharisees who heard it. This was no way for a father to behave. The son deserved punishment for his actions. They must have mocked and marveled at the foolish grace displayed by this loving father. But nothing could stop him from walking his son home.

I have often wondered what the first few hours and days were like for the prodigal son. It must have been a potent mixture of comfort and regret, brokenness and happiness. He was back at the family's table of great abundance and back under his father's protection. He now could live the life he was supposed to live, perhaps even live it better because he had experienced his father's grace. He now realizes the importance of being where he belongs.

This is what grace is all about. You and I are not saved *from* something as much as we are saved *for* something. God does not rescue us from the foreign lands of our rebellion and our self-imposed victimization without giving us a haven and a home where we can survive and prosper. It is not enough for our heavenly Father to make sure we are alive because of Him—He wants to make sure that we are in a place where we can thrive in Him. This requires a home. The lost son could not have what the Father intended for him until he was where the Father wanted him to be.

IT IS NOT ENOUGH FOR OUR HEAVENLY FATHER TO MAKE SURE WE ARE ALIVE BECAUSE OF HIM— HE WANTS TO MAKE SURE THAT WE ARE IN A PLACE WHERE WE CAN THRIVE IN HIM.

The Father is always watching and waiting for us to take the first step toward home. When we do, He runs to meet us, showers us with affection, and graciously walks us to our home in Him. In this new, loving environment, He places us under His protective canopy and gives us access to His resources. He takes away our shame. Now, we can become who He intends us to be.

OUR HOME IN HIM

I once had a little mixed breed dog named Charlie that had a passion for running away from home. We loved our dog, so he wore a collar with a tag listing our contact information. When he ran away, whoever found him could get our phone numbers off the tag and give us a call. We would rush out and bring Charlie home. That tag meant that Charlie was not homeless—he had a family and belonged to someone. The tag was his connection to his master and it ensured he would always make it home.

Unfortunately, one day, Charlie ran away right after we gave him a bath. His collar was not on, so anyone who found him had no way of knowing where his home was. He was lost in the worst way—not just lost from a geographical standpoint, but also from a relational standpoint. We eventually found Charlie and from then on, we kept a rein on his roaming ways.

When the prodigal son left his home and spent his inheritance in a distant land, he was not lost geographically, but spiritually and relationally. He knew his way back home, but he had walked away from who he was meant to be. He needed his relationship with his father, just as we need ours with God, our heavenly Father. When we walk away from the life He has given, the real damage is relational. Our *home* is our relationship with God. He is what your soul misses and what your heart longs for.

In the book of Acts, the apostle Paul is presented with an opportunity to explain the concept of our spiritual *home* in Jesus to a group of unbelieving Greeks in Athens. *"All the Athenians and the foreigners who lived there spent their time doing nothing but talking about and listening to the latest ideas"* (Acts 17:21 NIV). Given a platform there, Paul uses it to speak about our living God. He uses one of their idol-worshipping monuments as a springboard to unveil an important truth:

> *As I walked around and looked carefully at your objects of worship, I even found an altar with this inscription:* TO AN UNKNOWN GOD. *So you are ignorant of the very thing you worship—and this is what I am going to proclaim to you. The God who made the world and everything in it is the Lord of heaven and earth and does not live in temples built by human hands. And he is not served by human hands, as if he needed anything. Rather, he himself gives everyone life and breath and every-thing else…. For in him we live and move and have our being.*
>
> (Acts 17:23–25, 28 NIV)

Why would anyone follow or worship an *unknown* God, a God you cannot see? Because *in Him you live, you move, and you have your being.* We should be amazed, just as the Athenians were. Our home is in Him. He created us. He sustains us. He is the original fountain of life and He upholds us each moment. The reality that we live at all is His gift; our pro-longed existence is an expression of His love. Everything we are supposed to be is found in Him.

Elsewhere in the Bible, Paul tells us, *"God made him who had no sin to be sin for us, so that **in him** we might become the righteousness of God"* (2 Corinthians 5:21 NIV). Paul is saying you and I are not capable of mak-ing ourselves right with God, but *"in Him"* and through Him, we can become the very *"righteousness of God."* Righteousness is simply the God-given ability to do the right thing. Outside of Him, I constantly fail—in Him, I am given the ability to do what's right. Outside of Him, I can-not live the life that God has intended me to live. At best, I will just hang around the unredeemed edges. Like the prodigal son, I think I should live with the servants instead of with the Father. In Him, however, I fully find and enter my home. I receive all that the Father intended for me to have. And *in Him*, I am given right standing with the Father so I never have to be uncomfortable in His presence. In Him, I find all I need and everything I was ever meant to be.

In the gospel of John, Jesus explains the concept of *our home in Him.* Calling Himself the Vine and us the branches, He says, *"Remain in me, as I also remain in you. No branch can bear fruit by itself; it must remain in the vine. Neither can you bear fruit unless you remain in me"* (John 15:4 NIV). Just as a branch that's been cut off a vine is dead and barren, so are we lifeless without our attachment to Christ. In stark contrast, all of those who intentionally remain *"in the vine"* that is Jesus receive a life of abundance without limits. Jesus says, *"If you remain in me and my words remain in you, ask whatever you wish, and it will be done for you"* (John 15:7 NIV). The life you wish for, the life your soul knows you should have, is possible if you remain *in Him.*

OUTSIDE OF HIM, I CANNOT LIVE THE LIFE
THAT GOD HAS INTENDED ME TO LIVE. IN HIM,
HOWEVER, I FULLY FIND AND ENTER MY HOME.

This principle is rich and abundant throughout the New Testament. When you are spiritually identified and united with Christ, you are chosen, loved by God, redeemed, and forgiven. You are His child. In Him, you can be fruitful and whole. In Him, there is unlimited power to live the life that God divinely intended you to have. The *home* you have always longed for is *in Him* and He has everything you need.

A HOME WITHIN A HOME

Years ago, I was browsing in an airport bookstore and spotted a book about the worst places to live in America. As I glanced through its contents, I was surprised to see the town where I grew up on the list. I was offended…and weirdly proud at the same time. Offended that someone would be so judgmental of the place where I spent the first eighteen years of my life, and proud that the place I first called *home* helped to make me who I am today. For me, it wasn't some "worst place," but simply my home. My parents never asked me if I liked living there, nor was I ever given a map full of options. My opinion never influenced the place my family called home.

In our house, I only remember having control over one thing—the space in my bedroom. For a kid, having your own room is akin to owning a palace. A child's imagination can transform his room into anything he wants it to be. It's your own private world. As the youngest child, I had to wait to get my own room, but I finally got to live that dream. Eventually, I even took over the basement. As a teenager, it was like having my own little rent-free apartment. I was not in control of the city where we lived, the school I attended, or any other rooms in our home, but in the basement, I was king of the castle. Our house was my home, but my room was my private space, the place I could control.

You may not be in control of much in your own life. Maybe you're still a teenager. Maybe you're reading this in a rehab center or a prison. Maybe you're trapped by circumstances you can't control, or even by your choices. Maybe you're a working professional wearing a set of *golden handcuffs*, stuck in a career you don't like but can't afford to change. Maybe you feel like you're a prisoner to your debt to the point where your life feels more like slavery rather than destiny.

Whatever your situation, you may be wondering how to make a *home* when you have so little room to move. How can you progress into the future when the past still has you in its grip? How can you thrive where you are when the deck seems stacked against you and you do not even feel safe?

The answer is harsh, but hopeful. You must make a *home* within a *home*. You must erect a *home base*, a stronghold, right in the middle of where you find yourself—no matter how bad your situation is or seems to be. You take over a small portion of your life and you make that the starting place from which *God will build your new life*.

One of my favorite verses in the Bible is Psalm 23:5: "*You prepare a feast for me in the presence of my enemies. You honor me by anointing my head with oil. My cup overflows with blessings.*" When I am among my *enemies*, God prepares a *feast*! Whenever I read this verse, I always envision a gladiator type of battle. Swords are flying as terrible chaos and epic danger surrounds you. Enemies are coming at you from every direction. How could anyone survive?

But in the middle of all of that insanity, God comes down and sets a beautiful *feast* for you and Him. I imagine an intimate bistro table with a gourmet feast for two. You dine with your heavenly Father while the great battle rages around you. You sit, talk, and eat with God, your cup over- flowing. The battle does not affect the blessing. You are thriving and being refreshed. This is possible because God is bigger than your battle. The pic- ture created in that verse is profound and powerful. God can make *space* for you and Him where there seems to be none. God can make a *home* for you in Him even when you don't have your own room, even when you're not in control.

GOD CAN MAKE A *HOME* FOR YOU IN HIM EVEN WHEN YOU DON'T HAVE YOUR OWN ROOM, EVEN WHEN YOU'RE NOT IN CONTROL.

In the home I grew up in, I had space that I could call my own. At first, I did not value this gift. It was not really a *home within a home*, not a place where I acknowledged God or invited Him to spend time with me. He had great plans for me, but I didn't even know Him.

All of that changed in the fall of 1984. The same year I had my heart broken was the same year I had my heart restored, when I acknowledged the finished work of Jesus, His cross, and His resurrection. I asked Him to make a home in me and, in turn, He offered me a chance to make my home in Him.

Everything changed in me. I was transformed spiritually, mentally, and emotionally. But I still lived in the same city and in the same home. I could not do anything about that—but I *could* do a lot about what I did control. I decided that God's rightful place was to be the King of my *space*. I put Him in charge of the little I was controlling and He expanded my world.

I started getting up earlier so I could pray and read my Bible. Soon afterward, the change I experienced on the inside began expressing itself on the outside. My room was now His room. My space was now His space.

I started to get rid of anything that represented the *old me*. I cleaned up my room. The things that did not honor Him stood out like a sore thumb, so I got rid of all of it. After a while, my space became my own chapel of sorts. My bedroom became my personal sanctuary where I could get to know God. The place where I could hide from the world became a place where I would prepare to reach the world.

What I read and what I listened to evolved over the next few months and years. Later, my basement apartment became a bigger space for me to manage. Instead of abusing the freedom I was given, I used it to show God that I could be trusted with more. My basement was His basement. I spent some of my richest times with God in that basement. My big world was not changing much at all. But in my little world, everything was different. Even as I write this, I'm still amazed by the way God chose to grace my space with His presence.

During my travels, I'm occasionally a guest in someone's home. I always take that as a unique privilege, so I'm as polite as Mom taught me to be. I only do what I am invited to do. On the other hand, if I'm invited to *make myself at home*, I do just that! If my host says I should serve myself, then I head for the fridge. I may even sit in the best recliner and take over the remote.

The invitation is the key. Without it, I am far too polite to take any liberties. But with a kind invitation, I am far too polite not to make myself at home.

God is like that. God is a gentleman. He goes where He is invited. The good things He wants to give us require our kind and willing appeal. Your space can be His place. It all begins with your invitation.

OUR EXPANDING HOME

My little bedroom in my less-than-famous hometown is long gone. Our house was sold and resold. I still drive by it when I'm back that way. It seems so much smaller than I remember. The truth is, it *was* small. My life there was a good life, but it was not a big life. Things are now bigger and mostly better. My responsibilities these days are extensive and the spaces I manage, both literally and figuratively, dwarf what I used to have. The small rooms that were my place of preparation have expanded into the larger dwellings of my God-given assignments. God has allowed me to do more and be more.

The Bible embraces the tension between where we are and what we are called to do. God's plan always accounts for both your maturity and your mission. God knows precisely where you are and who you are, but He also has calculated all of your unrealized potential. You need to embrace your stage and grow while you dream. You have to be faithful when life is less than fruitful.

GOD'S PLAN ALWAYS ACCOUNTS FOR BOTH
YOUR MATURITY AND YOUR MISSION.
YOU NEED TO EMBRACE YOUR STAGE AND GROW
WHILE YOU DREAM.

These key concepts are on full display in another of Jesus's amazing stories: the parable of the *talents,* or the three servants, depending on the translation. (See Matthew 25:14–30.)

In this story, Jesus tells us about a master who's going away on a long journey, so he calls in three servants and entrusts them with a portion of his wealth. *"To one he gave five bags of gold, to another two bags, and to another one bag, each according to his ability"* (Matthew 25:15 NIV). Various translations say they are given talents, money, or bags of silver or gold. A *talent* in Jesus's time was a significant amount of money.

Notice the phrase *"each according to his ability."* Everyone has been gifted with unique ability. The point of this story is not how gifted we are, but rather how faithful we are with the gifts given to us. God never judges your ability compared to the abilities of others. We are judged according to what we have.

In this parable, the master sets off on his journey with the expectation that each servant will invest the money they have been given. The servants with five talents and two talents both double the master's money. They hustled, they worked hard, and they used their gifts to do the will of the master. But the servant with one talent played it safe. Out of fear, he buried his master's money to ensure he would not lose it. He did not invest his talent so it could grow.

When the master returns, he is so pleased with the first two servants for doubling his investment that he expands their territory and influence, giving them more to manage. But the third servant is called *wicked*, *lazy*, and *worthless* (verses 26, 30) and is thrown outside, "*into the darkness, where there will be weeping and gnashing of teeth*" (Matthew 25:30 NIV).

FAITHFULNESS HAS ITS REWARDS AND UNFAITHFULNESS HAS ITS CONSEQUENCES. WHEN YOU ARE FAITHFUL, DON'T BE SURPRISED IF GOD EXPANDS YOUR WORLD.

Faithfulness has its rewards and unfaithfulness has its consequences. When you are faithful, don't be surprised if God expands your world. Your *home*, your world, and your influence might be tiny at the moment, but God has His eyes on you. Everyone starts small, but no one starts with nothing. We all have been given a measure of talent and resources from our gracious Master. Start where you are, and if you are diligent and patient, you will be enriched. God will multiply your talents. God will faithfully expand your *home*.

This truth makes me think of my daughter, Jenna, who's gifted with musical talent. I'm often treated to a private concert when I'm home and it sometimes turns into a private worship service. Beautiful, raw melodies flow out of my daughter's bedroom and fill every corner of our home, with varying levels of anointed song. Jenna is preparing for something. The venues have not been booked, the dates aren't set, and no tickets are on sale— but she is passionately preparing for her future. Our home is her warm studio, where her small audience of overly proud parents celebrate every note. I try to provide her with everything she might need to reach her goal.

Home is a place where you can begin to invest in the gifts you have been given.

I think the lesson of the parable of the talents is *you have to bloom where you are planted*. You cannot wait for a better time or a better opportunity. God will not give us more if we refuse to use what we already have. No matter how limited your space or sphere of influence, you need to turn it into your studio of preparation. Bless the small audience who can hear you right now. Let the Master worry about *later*. Change what's in your grasp *now*. Your job is to thrive where you are. God will expand your *home* when the time is right.

DECORATED SHELTERS

I am a big fan of TV survival shows. I have watched so many of them that I am a bit of a survival expert. I love to think that if I was lost in the wilderness, I could build a cool survival shelter, start a fire without a match, locate a fresh water spring, trap my food, and eventually find my way out. I see myself as a survivor...but I wonder if I am. I like the *idea* of survival, but I hate the idea of being in any real danger. Maybe I could try to survive somewhere close to home, like the woods behind a grocery store. That way, if I was cold or hungry, I could go inside, warm up, and buy some snacks. Sounds like a plan I can get behind!

One thing I have never witnessed on a survival show is someone decorating their shelter. You don't care what Martha Stewart would think of your makeshift dwelling when you're trying to survive. You only care about the essentials. A survival shelter is not a home; it's just a temporary shack designed to keep you alive until you can get back to your real home.

Most people I meet are just surviving. They are lost in a place that is far from home. Yet they decorate and adorn their temporary habitat as if it were permanent. They act like they're home when they are still lost. Maybe the first step we must take toward home is to admit that we are not there yet. Eventually, we must ask ourselves, "Is this all there is? Is this home?"

This world offers us elaborate furnishings for our shelters. You can add a big-screen TV, a leather couch, and a refrigerator full of your favorite foods and drinks. You can become quite comfortable existing in a hollow environment. Your false narrative can eventually feel like a true story. But in your soul, in the depths of who you are, you know if you're home or not. Your heart always knows if you're just existing or really living.

IN YOUR SOUL, YOU KNOW IF YOU'RE HOME OR NOT. YOUR HEART ALWAYS KNOWS IF YOU'RE JUST EXISTING OR REALLY LIVING.

To find our way out of the wilderness, we must ruthlessly seek what God has intended for us. Other pursuits and distractions are as endless as the destinations we can type into a GPS. Sure, there are many places to visit, but most are not worth the trip. There is only one home for us and it's found in God. He has a good, pleasing, and perfect will for our lives. (See Romans 12:2.) God offers a place of perfection in Himself for me and you, a place where the search ends and we are finally home.

C. S. Lewis described it this way:

God made us: invented us as a man invents an engine. A car is made to run on gasoline, and it would not run properly on anything else. Now God designed the human machine to run on Himself. He Himself is the fuel our spirits were designed to burn, or the food our spirits were designed to feed on. There is no other.... God cannot give us a happiness and peace apart from Himself, because it is not there. There is no such thing.[3]

Outside of God, home is just a disappointing mirage. It's time to leave your makeshift survival shelter. It's time to come home.

3. C. S. Lewis, *Mere Christianity* (London: Geoffrey Bles, 1952).

DISCOVERY QUESTIONS

How does seeing God as a perfect Father affect you or change you?

_____

_____

_____

_____

Do you identify with the prodigal son? Why?

_____

_____

_____

_____

How can you apply your home in Christ to your daily life?

_____

_____

_____

_____

What talents has God given you? How is God telling you to use them?

_____

_____

_____

_____

PART II:

RESTORED

FOUR

SOUL-LEVEL HEALING

*Beloved, I pray that **you** may prosper in all things and be in health,
just as your **soul** prospers.*
—3 John 1:2 (NKJV)

One of my Bible college professors, Dr. Opal Reddin, may have been the most Christ-like person I ever met. I had the privilege of learning from her for a couple of semesters. She possessed great joy that flowed from her obvious love for Jesus; just being in her presence made you want to be closer to God. Many of us students affectionately called her "God's girlfriend." She seemed to have a connection with God that was over and above everyone else. When she prayed, heaven itself would saturate the room. When she spoke to you, the love of God would radiate through her. I have fond memories of the times we talked and the wisdom I gleaned from her. She is in my personal hall of fame of people I admire and want to emulate.

FOLLOWING SPIRITUAL GIANTS

If you were to choose the most influential person in your life, who would it be? It could be someone you've known personally or someone whose life has had a positive effect on you. Who is at the top of your *spiritual giant* list? Maybe it's Billy Graham or Mother Teresa. It might be a pastor or a grandparent who left a spiritual legacy for you to follow. You could even pick a person from the Bible, like the apostle Paul, King David, or Moses.

How about the apostle John? That would be a great choice. John's gospel gives us the most passionate account of Jesus's life. He is known as *the disciple who Jesus loved*. (See John 19:26.) He was one of the founders of the church, a spiritual giant who had a special connection with God.

What if John or your personal spiritual hero were standing in front of you right now? What would you talk to them about? If they offered to *pray* for you, what would you ask them to pray for? Would your requests be about your life, your family, your finances...or your walk with God? *Spiritual firepower* like this must be directed at what you think will impact your situation the most. Being granted access to someone with a direct line to heaven is not an everyday event for ordinary folks like you and me. You better think this through.

WHAT IF YOUR WELL-BEING IN ALL AREAS
DIRECTLY MIRRORED YOUR SOUL'S HEALTH?
WOULD YOU NEED AN AMBULANCE RIGHT AWAY?
OR WOULD YOU BE RICHLY BLESSED?

A moment like the one I am trying to illustrate sort of happened in John's letter to Gaius. He opens his masterpiece with a startling prayer for his dear friend: *"Beloved, I pray that you may prosper in all things and be in health, just as your soul prospers"* (3 John 1:2 NKJV). John doesn't give Gaius an opportunity to ask him to pray for what he needs. John just dives in with a prayer of blessing for his friend. I think he does this because no one would think to ask for *prosperity for their soul*. John makes his prayer conditional. In fact, he hinges everything on the condition of Gaius's soul.

When I study this prayer, I'm immediately drawn to the stuff about prospering in all things and being super healthy. Everyone wants those things. But John makes an astonishing transition when he uses the comparative phrase *just as*. John prays that Gaius's prosperity and health will equal his soul's prosperity. This is a contingent prayer of blessing. John is telling his friend that if he wants to improve the quality of his life, he must focus on the growth and flourishing of his soul.

No one would ask for that kind of prayer. Think about it: what if your whole life truly depended on the condition of your soul? What if your well-being in all areas—from your physical body to your relationships, work, career, finances, marriage, and everything else—directly mirrored your soul's health? Would you need an ambulance right away? Would you be bankrupt and homeless? Would you be in divorce court or friendless? Or would you be richly blessed? Would you *prosper even as your soul prospers?*

GOD'S PROSPERITY STARTS WITH THE *SOUL*. A THRIVING SOUL IS WHAT WILL LEAD YOU TO THE LIFE YOU ARE MEANT TO HAVE.

I am not sure that I would willingly ask John, Dr. Reddin, or anyone else to pray for me quite like that. But maybe that's just the kind of prayer we all need. Discovering the connection between your spiritual health and your physical life is a huge challenge, but it also gives us a life-altering breakthrough. It's so easy to get absorbed in the trivial, to be consumed by the temporary. Most of us chase the wrong things. We deprioritize what really matters and hurt ourselves in a multiplicity of ways. Perhaps John's prayer for Gaius's soul is the greatest prayer we can ever pray.

The struggle is real, isn't it? We want to be blessed, but we fail to understand the way God orders things. A blessed soul leads to a blessed life, not the other way around. This is a tough truth to embrace. It feels natural to think that prosperity in our lives will eventually lead to prosperity in our souls. *Yet the reverse is true.* God's prosperity starts with the *soul*. A thriving soul is what will lead you to the life you are meant to have.

MADE IN HIS IMAGE

When God was about to create man, He said, "*Let **Us** make man in **Our** image, according to **Our** likeness*" (Genesis 1:26 NKJV). Theologians believe that the plural pronouns in this verse, *Us* and *Our*, are the first scriptural reference to the Trinity. The word *trinity* encapsulates the fact that the Creator is one God in three distinctive persons: Father, Son, and Holy Spirit.

This subject has been debated for thousands of years; churches have split apart over it. I will give you just a few thoughts to consider. First, there are many Bible verses that refer to the three members of the Trinity at once, including Matthew 28:19, Luke 1:35, John 14:26, 2 Corinthians 13:14, Galatians 4:6, and Ephesians 1:17. All three Persons of the Trinity are present at the baptism of Jesus, including the Father, who spoke; the Holy Spirit, who appeared like a dove; and the Son. (See Matthew 3:16–17.) Jesus told us to baptize people "*in the name of the Father and the Son and the Holy Spirit*" (Matthew 28:19). Our God is a triune God.

When God created us in His image, He made us triune as well. His nature is represented in our nature. We too are made with three distinctive parts: the spirit, the soul, and the body. We live as a spirit, we have a soul, and we dwell in a body. Paul proclaims this trinity of man with these words: "*May the God of peace make you holy in every way, and may your whole **spirit** and **soul** and **body** be kept blameless until our Lord Jesus Christ comes again*" (1 Thessalonians 5:23).

You are a distinctive, three-part person made in the image of God Himself.

The *body* is the physical part of you, the outward expression of your being. It is through the body that we connect and communicate with the world through hearing, touch, sight, smell, and taste.

Paul said we should make our bodies *"a living and holy sacrifice"* to God (Romans 12:1); David praised God, acknowledging he was *"fearfully and wonderfully made"* by Him (Psalm 139:14 NKJV). God gave you a *body* so that His purposes in your life could be expressed in this physical world. But the only way for the *body* to be all it was meant to be is for it to submit itself fully to Jesus, along with the *spirit* and *soul*. You are meant to glorify God with all three parts of your being, including your body. All of you belongs to Him.

Referring to his body and how it changed when he found Christ, Paul wrote:

> *My old self has been crucified with Christ. It is no longer I who live, but Christ lives in me. So I live in this earthly **body** by trusting in the Son of God, who loved me and gave himself for me.*　　(Galatians 2:20)

Paul knew that his *old self*—the person he was before he met Jesus—wanted to have control over his *body*. His old self still wanted a way to express itself. This is why Paul made his body submit to the rule of his transformed *spirit*. Instead of letting his *body* dominate his life, he crucified his natural wants and lived by *"trusting in the Son of God."* His *spirit* and *soul* took precedence over his *body*. The *prosperity* of Paul's *soul* was on full display in the life Paul was living through his physical *body*. The *spiritual* dictated to the *natural*, not the other way around.

Now let's talk about the spirit and soul. They are closely related and work together...but they are not the same. They have mirroring qualities, but are distinct. At times, the Bible uses the terms *spirit* and *soul* interchangeably, but it also addressees them individually, as in this dynamic verse from Hebrews:

> *The word of God is alive and powerful. It is sharper than the sharpest two-edged sword, cutting between **soul** and **spirit**, between joint and marrow. It exposes our innermost thoughts and desires.*
> (Hebrews 4:12)

Your *spirit* is the spiritual part of you. When you experience salvation, it is your spirit that is regenerated or *born again* in Christ. Jesus declared, *"Truly, truly, I say to you, unless one is born of water and the Spirit, he cannot enter the kingdom of God"* (John 3:5 ESV). Salvation is a spiritual birth. Our spirits are made alive in Christ when we accept the finished work of His death on the cross and His resurrection. It is through spiritual birth that your spirit is awakened. You communicate with God through your spirit and it becomes the receptacle for hearing God's voice and receiving revelation. A regenerated *spirit* is the first step to living the life God meant for you to have.

YOU COMMUNICATE WITH GOD THROUGH
YOUR SPIRIT AND IT BECOMES THE RECEPTACLE
FOR HEARING GOD'S VOICE AND
RECEIVING REVELATION.

The *soul* is spiritual, but it's also emotional. It's the source of your imagination, creativity, and desires, and the seat of your conscience. Most theologians describe the soul as the place of our mind, will, and emotions. The Scriptures are rich with talk of the *soul* and full of metaphors that attempt to define it, but the description of our inner being is often vague.

Perhaps the soul is a spiritual mystery that can only be fully understood by God Himself. Yet His Word clearly tells us that your *soul* is vital to your interaction with God. Moses taught, *"If you search for [God] with all your heart and **soul**, you will find him"* (Deuteronomy 4:29). Jesus said, *"You must love the Lord your God with all your heart, all your **soul**, and all your mind. This is the first and greatest commandment"* (Matthew 22:37–38). Speaking to his own soul, the psalmist wrote, *"Why, my soul, are you downcast? Why so disturbed within me? Put your hope in God, for I will yet praise* *him, my Savior and my God"* (Psalm 42:11 NIV). The *soul* is a repetitive priority in the Scriptures' definition of you and the life God has for you.

THE ESSENCE OF WHO YOU ARE

Your *soul* is the essence of who you are. It is the fullest expression of your identity—spiritually, emotionally, and even mentally. You are really a *soul* that just happens to have a body. *"God formed Man out of dirt from the ground and blew into his nostrils the breath of life. The Man came alive—a living soul!"* (Genesis 2:7 MSG). *You* are your *soul*. This means you will never be who you are supposed to be unless you address yourself and your life at the *soul level.*

YOU ARE YOUR *SOUL*. YOU WILL NEVER BE WHO YOU ARE SUPPOSED TO BE UNLESS YOU ADDRESS YOURSELF AND YOUR LIFE AT THE *SOUL LEVEL*.

The Greek word for soul is *psuche*, from which we get the words psyche and psychology. Your *psyche*, or your mentality, is ultimately a living representation of your *soul*. How you think and feel about yourself and your life is a *soulful* thing. God wants you to have a healthy soul because that will lead to a healthy mentality, which will produce a healthy life.

Here is the primary problem that many of us face: we may have experienced a *spiritual birth*, but we still have an *injured soul*. We are regenerated spiritually, but we are still wounded emotionally and mentally. We experience an overflow of soul-level change when the spirit is awakened at salvation, but we often need restoration and healing on the other side of that transformation. The deep inner wounds of the past do not always magically disappear when we are saved.

These *soul wounds* and their impact vary for everyone. If only we could all come to Christ at a young age and avoid the damage created by a life apart from salvation! But we live in a broken world filled with jagged edges that tear at our tender souls. The good news is God wants us whole. He wants us to be healed at the deepest level. He knows how to perform surgery on our souls.

HERE IS THE PRIMARY PROBLEM THAT MANY OF US FACE: WE MAY HAVE EXPERIENCED A *SPIRITUAL BIRTH*, BUT WE STILL HAVE AN *INJURED SOUL*.

David proclaimed, *"He restores my soul"* (Psalm 23:3 ESV). To *restore* something is to bring it back to its original, intended condition and purpose. God doesn't simply want to improve your condition; He wants to change your entire nature! God wants to *restore* you so you can experience the plans He has for your life. God knows who you're supposed to be and He has a vision for your restoration. When your soul is restored, you can stop pretending to be who you want to be and start being *who you really are*. The river of your identity can flow from the deepest of sources. You can have a purpose and a persona that emanate from a healthy, restored soul.

THE FULLNESS OF YOUR REDEMPTION

I'm writing this chapter in the living room of our home. When we moved here, we wondered if it would be too big for us. Two of my kids are married now and there are only three of us here. But as I suspected, we use every inch of this space. Every room, nook, and cranny are utilized on a regular basis.

The wood-burning fireplace just might be my favorite feature in this house. We had some pretty cold days in Missouri this past winter, which rekindled my love for the pure warmth of a classic hearth fire.

I was talking about fireplaces with some friends of ours at a Christmas party and they said something really funny. They had just discovered that they could burn wood in their fireplace! After many years of sitting empty and unused, suddenly, their fireplace brings them warmth and delight. They now comfort themselves with enchanting wood fires every chance they get.

WHEN YOUR SOUL IS RESTORED, YOU CAN STOP PRETENDING TO BE WHO YOU WANT TO BE AND START BEING *WHO YOU REALLY ARE.*

Imagine that! Your expensive home has an amazing feature and you never use it because you didn't know you could. My overactive imagination takes this scenario even further. What if they had failed to discover an automatic garage door...or a spare bedroom...or a finished basement? What if suddenly this summer, they found out they had a beautiful deck and barbecue grill? Then, wouldn't they be surprised by the sparkling blue water of their backyard pool? How could they have missed it? A whole new world of family fun can now begin!

The real tragedy would be the wasted time that could have been spent enjoying the abundance of what was already theirs. Of course, no one could miss the features of their *home* like that.

Or could they?

Think of your relationship with Jesus like an elaborate house in which you have been given more than you can begin to comprehend. The *home* you have in Christ is filled with pleasure, benefits, and mysteries that deserve your discovery and enjoyment. In our Father's house, there are all kinds of *spiritual features* that meet our every need and fulfill us at our deepest levels. Paul proclaims that God the Father *"has blessed us with every spiritual blessing in the heavenly realms because we are united with Christ"*

(Ephesians 1:3). When we make our *home* in Christ, everything we need is available to us. The only question is: will we take advantage of what He has provided? You could be warming yourself by the *fireplace* of His abundant love right now! You really should take a curious stroll around the *home* that His generous grace has provided for you. Today is a great day to start discovering all that you have been given.

WHEN WE MAKE OUR *HOME* IN CHRIST, EVERYTHING WE NEED IS AVAILABLE TO US. THE ONLY QUESTION IS: WILL WE TAKE ADVANTAGE OF WHAT HE HAS PROVIDED?

When most people hear the word *redemption*, they have an incomplete idea of what it means. They might know it's a religious term; they might even realize it has something to do with the cross of Christ. But most fail to recognize what I call the *fullness of their redemption*. To *redeem* is to buy back something that was lost. The Bible says, *"God bought you with a high price"* (1 Corinthians 6:20). The paid price was the blood of Jesus poured out on the cross as a sacrifice to God to atone for man's sin. God bankrupted heaven so you and I could have a chance to live the life He intends for us to have. Paul's words to Titus offer a great summation for this point:

> ...*Christ Jesus, who [willingly] gave Himself [to be crucified] on our behalf to redeem us and purchase our freedom from all wickedness, and to purify for Himself a chosen and very special people to be His own possession, who are enthusiastic for doing what is good.*
>
> (Titus 2:13–14 AMP)

Focus on the last phrase: *"who are enthusiastic for doing what is good."* Redemption is something God does *for you* to equip you to do something *for Him.* He redeems with a purpose in mind. We have been redeemed, forgiven of our debt of sin, but also chosen *"for doing what is good."* Your redemption is not something you simply obtain; it's something you get to live out.

THE REDEMPTIVE EVENT

Let me explain. For just a minute, I want you to think about the massive price that Jesus paid for you. Jesus dying on the cross for your sins can sound like an *action,* but it was really an *event.* Bible scholars believe that the actual events on the cross took around eight hours to complete. The Scriptures tell us that He was crucified at the third hour (see Mark 15:25), which would have been about 9 a.m. Darkness covered the land from the sixth hour, noon, until the ninth hour or 3 p.m., when Jesus cried out to His Father from the cross just before His death. (See Mark 15:33–24; Matthew 27:45–46; Luke 23:44–46.)

From the time Jesus was crucified until the time He died was at least six hours. But what about the events before the cross—His betrayal, His beating, and His corrupt trial? We can add at least two hours to the *event* for the torture Jesus experienced before He was nailed to the cross. The cross was not *a single act*—it was *a redemptive event.*

This *event of the cross* becomes even more severe and gut-wrenching when you consider other excruciating aspects of what Jesus went through. How about the fact that He was crucified naked? That forced humiliation is surely a form of abuse. What about the desertion of most of His closest friends and followers? This abandonment while He was on the cross led to the most profound loneliness any human being has ever experienced. The Bible also tells us that those who passed by *"hurled insults"* at Jesus (see Matthew 27:39 NIV), wounding Him with their words.

We also know that Jesus was spit upon and punched in the face. The hair of His beard was pulled out. He was savagely whipped thirty-nine times with a tool of torture that was designed to rip His flesh from His body.

We could go on and on, describing the price Jesus paid for us with unrelenting detail. The cross took time—excruciating time. The *cross* was an *event* with layers of pain. And all the pain was for a purpose: for your redemption and mine.

THE FULLNESS OF YOUR *REDEMPTION PACKAGE* WAS PROVIDED BY THE TOTALITY OF JESUS'S SACRIFICE. HE GAVE UP HIS LIFE SO YOU COULD HAVE THE LIFE HE HAS DESTINED FOR YOU.

Why is it so critical that we examine the entire scope of what Jesus suffered? The answer is enlightening and powerful. The event of the cross is directly connected to what Jesus provides for us. The fullness of your *redemption package* was provided by the totality of His sacrifice. Every millisecond of hurt and torture that Jesus went through *was and is* redemptive. He paid every price so that He could provide something for you. He gave up His life so you could have the life He has destined for you. He went through each aspect of torture so He could redeem (pay the price) for something He wants you to have. His suffering systemically restored your ability to live the life you are destined to live. His pain is the foundation for your purpose.

How do we apply the truth of our redemption to our daily lives? First, let's consider the effect of damaging words. Every hurtful thing that is ever said about us and all *verbal wounds* we have experienced were taken on the cross by Christ. When the crowd abused Him with their words, He was paying a redemptive price for our healing. Jesus even took to the cross any negative words we have ever said about ourselves! *You are redeemed.* That is your current status, no matter what others might say or think.

The power of our redemption applies to many other areas of our lives. All of the damage from my sins and the sins of others toward me was taken to the cross by Jesus. Isaiah tells us:

He was pierced for our rebellion, crushed for our sins. He was beaten so we could be whole. He was whipped so we could be healed…. The LORD *laid on him the sins of us all.* (Isaiah 53:5–6)

There is forgiveness of sin in our *redemption package* but there is also *wholeness* and *healing*. When His tormenters exposed Him and abused Him, Jesus was redeeming us from the damage of our abuse. When they abandoned Him, He was redeeming us from all of the abandonments we have or ever will experience.

The cross was all for *you*—for every one of us. Your redemption is comprehensive and complete. All that you have done and all that was done to you was redeemed by Christ through the event of the cross. Colossians 2:9–10 (NIV) proclaims: *"In Christ all the fullness of the Deity exists in bodily form, and in Christ you have been brought to fullness."* This is the miracle you have been given in Christ; His fullness is now your fullness. You no longer have to be incomplete.

THE POWER OF A STEP

A few years ago, I was a part of a group of pastors who climbed Half Dome together. This mountain sits at nearly 9,000 feet in elevation in the middle of beautiful Yosemite National Park in California. The average hike to Half Dome is about fourteen miles round trip, which takes all day, from daylight to nightfall, even in the summertime. It takes roughly 2,000 steps to walk a mile, so my hike at Half Dome was about 28,000 steps on mostly rough terrain and at a steep elevation.

For me, the trip was a last-minute invite, so I had not trained for it. I woke up the morning of the hike and wondered what I had got myself into. But I took a step…actually, I took 28,000 of them. Those steps led me to where I needed to be. I did make it to the top, but just barely.

If I called you up right now and asked you to climb Half Dome with me, would you do it? Someone young, fit, and adventurous would most likely say yes. But what if you're older, out of shape, or both? What if you have some physical limitations and you just could not attempt such a climb? Maybe you're afraid of heights, or you're too cautious to do something that's potentially dangerous.

The daunting nature of a task can keep us from taking the first step. When the mountain is high, the biggest challenge is getting started. The start is always the scariest part.

Let's change my hypothetical request for just a minute. Maybe I call you and simply ask if you are willing to take one step with me, or perhaps just three or four. Most people can do that. When I was gaining the courage to write this book, I read a tweet by an author that went something like this: "If you can write a word, then you can probably write a sentence. If you can write a sentence, then you can write a paragraph. If you can write a paragraph, you can write a chapter. Repeat that and you can write a book."

A book seemed like a mountain that was too high to climb, but when I thought of it as a collection of sentences, I was suddenly motivated. Maybe a *mile* is just 2,000 small steps that have ganged up and are now trying to look scary! But one small step by itself is not intimidating at all.

The truth is, none of us can climb a mountain all at once, but if we muster the courage to take one step and then another, there is no peak that's beyond our reach.

WHEN WE THINK WE WILL NEVER BE ABLE TO CLIMB OUR WAY UP TO THE LIFE GOD INTENDED FOR US, WE MUST FOCUS ON *STEPS*.

As I write this book, I'm trying to feel what you're feeling. I imagine that reading about *soul-level healing* might resemble an invitation to *climb*

a mountain. Most of us are intimidated by the *heights* and *depths* of our issues. We think we will never be able to climb our way up to the life God intended for us. The mountain just seems too big. So we must focus on *steps* instead of *arrivals.* If you start taking some steps, eventually, you will arrive. Every journey begins and ends with a step. David prayed, *"Guide my steps by your word"* (Psalm 119:133). Paul wrote, *"Since we are living by the Spirit, let us follow the Spirit's leading in every part of our lives"* (Galatians 5:25). The Holy Spirit has a path for you out of your pain. He wants to guide your steps.

FOUR SMALL STEPS

In my thirty years of helping wounded people, I've noticed a well-established pattern. Time and time again, I have witnessed the powerful effect that *four small steps* can have on any broken life. They are simple, yet game-changing. These steps are: authenticity, access, appropriation, and acceptance. Let me break that down for you:

AUTHENTICITY: BE HONEST!

THE WORST THING YOU CAN DO ABOUT YOUR BROKENNESS IS LIE TO YOURSELF OR OTHERS ABOUT IT. PRETENSE IS POISON TO THE *SOUL.*

The worst thing you can do about your brokenness is lie to yourself or others about it. Pretense is poison to the *soul.* I'm not suggesting that you shout your issues from the rooftops or make them a focus of every conversation, but I *am* proposing that you become vulnerable in the most authentic way. This begins with an honest, personal assessment of what and who hurt you. You yourself will be on the list of offenders, for sure, as all of us possess self-inflicted damage.

I have laid out four small steps here because they point in the direction of your healing.

You can expect the enemy to fight against your progress. He is fine with you being *active*, but meaningful movement terrifies him. The devil has no problem with momentum in your life, just as long as it's not in the direction of Jesus. In the lives of wounded people—which is basically all of us—the devil's primary tactic is to prolong their pain by keeping them distracted. He wants us to chase false solutions that comfort the emotions, but do not affect the soul.

Recognize the difference between progress and pacification. Your soul doesn't need cheap comforts. It needs the healing power of Jesus—healing that reaches the core of your being.

DISCOVERY QUESTIONS

Who is at the top of your spiritual giant list? Why?

_____

_____

_____

_____

_____

What would your life be like if it was tied directly to the health of your soul?

_____

_____

_____

_____

_____

How does God's nature represent itself in ours?

_____

_____

_____

_____

_____

Which of the four steps of healing your soul wounds did you identify with the most? Why?

_____

_____

_____

_____

_____

FIVE

BACK TO EDEN

*The LORD God said, "It is not good for the man to be alone.
I will make a helper suitable for him."*
—Genesis 2:18 (NIV)

Her name was Stacy and she was from Alabama. It was the first day of my fifth year at Webster Elementary School and Stacy was the first person I noticed. She was the most beautiful girl I had seen in my ten years of life. In my infatuated mind, her alluring southern accent sounded like music. I was hooked on her right from the beginning. (This must be where my love for Alabama girls began because I ultimately would marry one. My wife, Jeanne, is from Alabama—and she is way prettier than Stacy was.)

I fell deeply in love with Stacy during the first few months of fifth grade. There was just one problem: I was too scared and too shy to talk to her! I think I may have kicked dirt on her at recess once, a sure sign of elementary school love. But that was about it. Days turned into weeks, weeks turned into months, and finally, the school year was over. Stacy was in a different class for sixth grade, so I didn't see her much. But then came middle school.

As God had surely designed it, Stacy and I ended up in the same middle school. Never mind that our town only *had* one middle school, I still think providence brought us together *again*! Seeing Stacy after a long summer made my young heart beat faster, but something else pushed me past my shyness. Something called a *spiral perm*! It was 1980 and this iconic new hairstyle was sweeping the nation. Stacy's beauty, crowned by her new hairstyle, was simply too much for my heart to take. So I approached my friend Ben and asked him what to do. I'm not sure why I chose Ben, but maybe his thirteen-year-old mind would have some wisdom for me.

With great conviction, Ben told me I should write a note to Stacy, telling her how I felt. It *sounded* like a good idea. My inspiration exploded into my spiral notebook as I crafted a note that would rival the world's great poets. It was dripping with pure romance. Stacy would not be able to resist.

SHE CHECKED THE YES BOX!

I still have my *work of art* memorized: "Dear Stacy, do you like me? I like you. Would you like to go with me?" Back in the day, if you were with someone, you were *going* with each other. I'm not sure where we were *going* since neither one of us could drive! In a stroke of pure brilliance, I decided to make it easy for Stacy to respond to my note. I placed three boxes on the page after my written offer of affection: a big box for *yes*, a smaller box for *maybe*, and an almost microscopic box for *no*. I folded up the note that contained my hopes and dreams and courageously handed it to Stacy. Later that day, she gave it back to me with the *yes* box clearly checked. It was on! She had voted yes to our love and now we were *going together*.

Unfortunately, it took me about three weeks to know what to do with my newfound status. I never even spoke to her. In fact, I *avoided* her. To say that I was overwhelmed and frightened is an understatement. When I finally did approach her, my insecurity made the relationship so awkward that it only lasted one day. She broke up with me. Just like that, one of the great love stories of our tender school years was over. As funny as it is to think of now, I do remember feeling real pain and regret when it ended. I could not understand why I failed to engage with her and why my fears outweighed my desires. It would be many years later before I would even begin to address my underlying issues. But now I know that the river of my dysfunction ran deeper than I ever could have imagined.

I think we all have a *Stacy story*. We all have memories of self-sabotaging our lives and robbing ourselves of something good. You can probably think of many things that your insecurities, fears, and impaired thinking have stolen from you. Maybe the list is longer than you care to admit; I know mine is. You probably have a history of getting in your own way and it has been like that for as long as you can remember. We often wound our souls unintentionally. This can manifest itself in many areas, but it is more prevalent and more painful in the realm of relationships. People you care about check the *yes* box and you are so excited, but then you become your own worst enemy. You rob yourself of something that could have been wonderful. Sometimes, it is not your fault, but too many times, it is. Even worse, this tragedy is repetitive, a cycle that you have no idea how to escape. *Been there, done that, I never want to go back.* The good news is, you don't have to. There *is* a better way.

THE LIFE GOD WANTS YOU TO HAVE IS NOT JUST ABOUT *WHAT* YOU ARE CALLED TO DO; IT'S ABOUT *WHO* YOU ARE CALLED TO DO IT WITH.

It's impossible to address the life God intends for us to have without talking about relationships. God desires a rich and abundant life for you. It's not supposed to be a lonely existence. Relationships add pleasure to your purpose. The life God wants you to have is not just about *what* you are called to do; it's about *who* you are called to do it with. The people accompanying you make your journey enjoyable at the deepest levels. God has more for your relational life than a trail of hurt and brokenness. Real restoration in you creates a chain reaction that transforms your ability to connect with others. The history of your relationships may read more like a horror story than a romance novel, but your story is not over. God is not done. In fact, I believe God is going to write a *new relational chapter* in your future that overwhelms your hurtful history. Check your own *yes* box because your new love story is just beginning.

LONGING FOR HOME

I travel a lot. I can handle short trips of three to five days easily and not get too homesick, but after a week or so on the road, I begin to *long* for home. I miss simple things that are dear to me—sleeping in my bed, sitting in my favorite chair, holding my wife's hand, playing with my dog, eating cereal out of my usual bowl. When I am gone for an extended period of time, I even start experiencing *associations*. Every sensation, sight, smell, taste, and sound causes me to think of my family and miss what I used to have. Things just will not be *right* in my world until I'm finally heading back home.

When my life was transformed by Jesus at the age of sixteen, I began to experience some strange longings. I wanted something that I had no memory of, something I could not put into words. I felt a desire to get back to *something* I had never possessed. I felt I was missing something, but I didn't know what it was. This makes no sense, I know, but even so, I bet you have felt those longings, too. You have desired a life and an existence that you cannot even begin to describe. You desire something *more* than you've ever had and you *yearn* for what your soul knows you are missing.

This mysterious desire is awakened in all of us when our spirits are transformed at salvation. It is a God-given longing for a life and relationships that display what Christ has done in us. It has its own energy because this desire comes from the Holy Spirit. God wants you to want what He has for you. What I am talking about are *echoes of the soul.* These longings are like *flashing signals* in the heart of a Christ follower. They are pulling you away from a lesser life that is no longer your home. It is the deep calling to deep. (See Psalm 42:7.) It is your soul reaching out to the living God. It is the unquenchable knowledge that God has something more, something better, for you.

As I mentioned earlier, my heritage and my home, at least for the first eighteen years of my life, was Granite City, Illinois. I will always have both good and bad memories of that city. It's changed a lot since I lived there. Schools have closed, new businesses have opened, and new people have moved in. Almost a generation has gone by. But the memories in my head are timeless.

We can understand memories because we all have them. We all have associations that are carved into our psyches by experiences. But how can we remember or long for a place that we have never experienced?

YOU HAVE A SPIRITUAL HERITAGE THAT YOUR SOUL IS FAMILIAR WITH. YOUR SPIRIT IS AWAKENED TO THIS REALITY WHEN IT IS MADE ALIVE IN CHRIST.

The answer is profound. You have a spiritual heritage that your soul is familiar with. Whether you realize it or not, you are connected and affected by a past that you are now a part of. Your spirit is awakened to this reality when it is made alive in Christ. You begin to long for what you should have because now in Christ, it is possible to have it. Your soul becomes curious about its original past when you start to dream of your God-given future.

Our original home was a place named Eden. When God first created man, He placed him in this garden of perfection, an extreme paradise. The Bible says all of the trees in Eden *were pleasing to the eye and good for food"* (Genesis 2:9 NIV). Man was given a purpose: to take care of the garden and give names to all of the animals. (See Genesis 2:15, 19.) How awesome that must have been! Best of all, man had intimate fellowship with God. There were no barriers between creation and Creator. There was no sin, nor the insecurity it fosters. This home was perfection.

Well, almost. This *perfect home* only lacked one thing: human relationship. *"The LORD God said, 'It is not good for the man to be alone. I will make a helper suitable for him'"* (Genesis 2:18 NIV). The great Creator resolved

Adam's seclusion by causing him to fall into a deep sleep while He crafted the *woman* of His new creation. (See Genesis 2:21–22.) God Himself inaugurates the plan of a loving relationship. This was and is the beginning. Man had the ultimate environment to thrive in; he had purpose and he had his Creator, but something was missing. God saw a relational void in His creation and He filled it by making woman. Perfection was made even more perfect.

The Bible records what I believe was Adam's God-given reaction: "*This is now bone of my bones and flesh of my flesh; she shall be called 'woman,' for she was taken out of man*" (Genesis 2:23 NIV). Adam recognizes that they are of the same essence; he knows that the woman originated with him. An intimacy that was unavailable before is now possible. The next verse declares it: "*That is why a man leaves his father and mother and is united to his wife, and they become one flesh*" (Genesis 2:24 NIV). The *Living Bible* puts it this way: "*The two become one person.*" What beautiful language! No wonder we hear these phrases at virtually every wedding. Relationships are a product of creation, not an invention of culture. Eden is the place where our love stories began.

OUR VERY SOULS KNOW WE NO LONGER LIVE IN
THE TRANQUILITY OF EDEN. WE KNOW THERE IS
SOMETHING MISSING—AND WE WANT IT BACK!

Our longing for home is more than an inner lament over the messed-up world we live in. These desires are deeper than our regrets. Our very souls know we no longer live in the tranquility of Eden. We know there is something missing—and we want it back! Our deepest desires are for the beautiful intimacy that we have lost. We want God to declare that the aloneness we feel is "*not good.*" We dream that He could create a life for us that fills the relational void. He sees these desires like He hears our prayers. He longs to give us what we should have never lost.

PARADISE LOST

We are not given much insight into the days, months, or years that Adam and Eve spent together in the garden of Eden. But we *do* know they were *"naked and were not ashamed"* (Genesis 2:25 ESV). God could have told us many things about the first love story in the history of the world, but He chose one potent pronouncement that echoes with implication: Adam and Eve were *naked but not ashamed*. Where is all the material for future romance novels or rom-com movies? How about highlighting a lovely walk by the headwaters of the Euphrates or a dinner beneath the stars? All we get is they were naked and they were okay with it?

It may be frustrating for anyone looking for a good romance, but there is a divine purpose in the brevity of those few words. In one short sentence, Genesis 2:25 highlights for us the two ingredients that make loving relationships thrive. The reference to nakedness points to a sense of vulnerability. The lack of shame speaks to the absence of insecurity. There was no doubt or uncertainty in them because such a feeling did not yet exist.

Can you imagine the pure intimacy of a relationship where you're totally *vulnerable* and *secure* at the same time? Neither can I. We have no idea what that would look like because everyone purposely avoids vulnerability. We all are cursed with some form of insecurity that hinders our relationships. That's why a spiral perm was enough to get my twelve-year-old self to write a note...but it was not enough to actually foster a relationship. I avoided vulnerability and my insecurities sabotaged me before my love could even begin to know me. This is common problem for all of us. But Adam and Eve once had something better—something perfect.

Some time ago, I bought a new car. It was gorgeous, it purred, and the paint and body were flawless. I was so cautious with it that I could barely enjoy owning it. I was almost relieved when the first dings and scratches showed up. Why are we that way? Our damaged selves unwittingly want everything around us to be scarred like we are. It seems that our fallen natures are always uncomfortable with perfection.

I think this trait began with Adam and Eve. Think about it: they are experiencing the best possible circumstances. They are created for each other, sin did not exist, and they are walking in unity with God. They have a perfect environment, a perfect relationship with God and each other. There is no sickness or pain of any kind. Why would they mess with this level of perfection? But they did. Just like you and me, they sabotaged themselves.

OUR DAMAGED SELVES UNWITTINGLY
WANT EVERYTHING AROUND US TO BE SCARRED
LIKE WE ARE. IT SEEMS THAT OUR
FALLEN NATURES ARE ALWAYS UNCOMFORTABLE
WITH PERFECTION.

I have a hard time with this part of the story of creation. God created both Eden and mankind. Why would He allow for any possibility of destroying what He created? God allows man to partake of everything Eden has to offer...except for just one thing.

> And the LORD God commanded the man, "You are free to eat from any tree in the garden; but you must not eat from the tree of the knowledge of good and evil, for when you eat from it you will certainly die."
> (Genesis 2:16–17 NIV)

There it is—a tree that leads to tragedy. A way to mess things up, a poison that can end perfection. *Why would God allow it?* This is a valid question, but the answer is painfully obvious.

GOD'S GIFT OF FREE WILL

Real love cannot be forced. If there was no way out of the covenant love God has with His creation, the willing relationship would turn into a form of slavery. God gifted mankind with free will, which means Adam and Eve could live for Him and each other by authentic choice...or not. Unfortunately, they chose not to and they lost everything.

Put yourself in the garden with them for a minute. You're living in wondrous paradise and there is only one way to mess it up. Nature's banquet surrounds you, but there's just one tree your loving Creator has told you to avoid. Wouldn't you do everything in your power to stay away from it? Wouldn't you train some lions to roar out a warning when you got too close to that tree, or dig a moat around it with crocodiles in it? Instead, we see mankind flirting with disaster. They are *near* the tree, talking to a lying serpent. (See Genesis 3:1–6.)

The devil, disguised as a serpent, lies to Eve, convincing her to try the fruit, which she then shares with Adam. The infection of sin taints the pure perfection of their world. Paradise is lost. What happens next blows me away.

At that moment their eyes were opened, and they suddenly felt shame at their nakedness. So they sewed fig leaves together to cover them-selves. (Genesis 3:7)

They immediately transitioned from *naked but unashamed* to "Oh, my goodness, we are *naked*! We better cover up." Shame is birthed in this moment; it did not exist before, but now it does. Can you imagine what this felt like? They have never known anything but love and perfect intimacy with God, each other, and their surroundings, and now they're suddenly flooded with *shame*. They are feeling what we feel. It must have been terrifying.

Shame is the worst form of insecurity there is. It makes you feel so worthless that you hide in fear. It's a deeper, rawer emotion than guilt because it turns your sin into your identity. When sin entered the world, mankind became fearful and ashamed. Sin always includes fear as part of its destructive package.

Before this point, Adam and Eve's love story seemed foreign and unattainable. They were breathing the rarest of air and living in the relational perfection we long for but can never seem to experience.

But in Genesis 3:7, they are feeling the fear that we carry within us today, experiencing the same insecurity that permeates our very identities. It's easier to relate to them now, isn't it? Now, they are covering up because they're ashamed. Now, they are afraid like us. And it gets worse.

That evening, God walks into the garden, looking for them. They are hiding in fear because they have a full realization of their nakedness. (See Genesis 3:10.) God's unsolicited response speaks volumes: *"Who told you that you were naked?"* (Genesis 3:11). God knows their innocence has been broken and insecurity has replaced their purity. They have knowledge now, but it is not good knowledge. They have experience now, but it is the worst kind. Their newfound enlightenment has devastated their very souls.

IT'S INTERESTING THAT THE ENEMY'S LURE WAS THAT *"YOUR EYES WILL BE OPENED."* HE DECEIVES THEM INTO BELIEVING THAT THEIR PERFECTION WAS MISSING SOMETHING. THIS IS A PROBLEM THAT STILL EXISTS TODAY.

It's interesting that the enemy's lure was that *"your eyes will be opened"* (Genesis 3:5). He deceives them into believing that their perfection was missing something. This is a problem that still exists today. We want what we should not have, what we were not designed to have. We want to know everything…except for what we really need. God was not hiding anything from Adam and Eve; He was protecting them from harm. He had introduced them to Himself, each other, and His reason for creating them. Knowledge of their nakedness was immaterial. It would not add value to their lives. God made them pure for their own protection.

I find the next action in this broken love story to be the most tragic. Sadly, I can relate to it on a personal level. God asks them if they have eaten fruit from the forbidden tree and Adam says, *"It was the woman you gave me who gave me the fruit, and I ate it"* (Genesis 3:12). The destruction of paradise is happening so fast, we can barely keep up. We see the massive consequence of sin: fear, shame, insecurity, broken intimacy, and now, here comes relational destruction. Adam quickly throws Eve under the bus. His newfound insecurity lashes out and hurts someone he loves. Now we know why the garden of Eden feels so familiar to our souls. This is not just the place we long for, but also the place where we lost what we should have had. God invented a loving relationship with this couple and they're also the prototype of its demise. We can relate to this story because we are related to *them*. We are all sons and daughters of Adam and Eve and we have inherited what they passed down. What was in them is now in us.

OUR BENT NATURES

To say that we have inherited the consequences of what happened in Eden is a huge concept. Theologians call this the "the doctrine of original sin," meaning the sin of Adam and Eve has been transmitted into the very nature of all mankind. What happened there is still affecting us here. More than a few verses in the Bible speak to this reality. Psalm 51:5 states that we all come into the world as sinners: *"Behold, I was brought forth in iniquity, and in sin my mother conceived me"* (NKJV). Paul says all people who are not in Christ are *"sons of disobedience"* and we are all *"by nature children of wrath"* (Ephesians 2:2–3 ESV). Back in the book of Genesis, we are told, *"The intention of man's heart is evil from his youth"* (Genesis 8:21 ESV).

The Scriptures are clear and comprehensive: we all are natural-born sinners, damaged by the sinful fall of the first two people in Eden.

If you find this concept hard to believe, then you probably need to hang out with a toddler. Ever notice how selfish young children can be and how often they lie, cheat, or steal? No one had to teach them these behaviors.

By the time we reach *the terrible twos*, our sin nature surfaces. It's painfully obvious that evil behavior comes natural to all of us at every age. We are all born with natures that are prone toward sin. Just as we long for the days of perfection in the garden of Eden, we are haunted by the consequences of the first couple's sin. Our souls have been mangled and twisted by our connection to Eden. Like a car with a bent axle, we are helplessly steered in the direction of the weaknesses that their fall created. From the very start, our lives lean toward the lies Adam and Eve fell for. We are born predisposed to insecurity. The Eden we are trying to get back to is also the place that we cannot escape from.

JUST AS WE LONG FOR THE DAYS OF PERFECTION IN THE GARDEN OF EDEN, WE ARE HAUNTED BY THE CONSEQUENCES OF THE FIRST COUPLE'S SIN.

Why is this important? What value is there in understanding the unbreakable connection we have with a place called Eden? The answer to this question has the power to transform you and set your life on a new course. Your understanding of Eden is critical because to change your *behavior* you must deal with your *nature*. We were all born with a relentless tendency toward something less than we were created for. Our natures have positioned us away from who we were meant to be. Adam and Eve chose less than what could have been and now, you and I tragically repeat their pattern. The deck has been stacked against us. It turns out that our defeat was an inside job.

Now, if you grew up in a Christ-honoring family, where you are introduced to the redemption offered in Christ at an early age, the fall could have a milder impact on you. But we all eventually come face to face with our inherited fallen natures. What you do with this reality will determine whether you live the life God wants you to have...or not. If you keep dealing with the *outward* part of your life without addressing the *inward* forces that are holding you back, then real victory will always elude you. You will lose over and over again because you fail to address the true source of your defeat: the enemy within. This is why Jesus always starts with our hearts. His power is the one force in the universe that can win the *nature* war that began in Eden.

THE DOG DAYS ARE OVER

We have always had a dog. Dogs become like members of the family. You love them and you truly believe that they love you back. But you must be careful to remember that they are not human. *A dog is a dog.* This is the wisdom I imparted to my wife and kids over the years. Even a great dog will bite you if you mess with it while it's eating. Our wonderful dogs have been known to eat out of the trash can, drink out of the toilet, and lick the dirty plates in the dishwasher. You can train a dog, but you cannot change its nature.

The great news for us is that unlike dogs, our natures can be changed in Christ. In his second letter, Peter wrote, "*God has given us everything we need for living a godly life*" (2 Peter 1:3). In the very next verse, he assures us, "*He has given us great and precious promises…to share his divine nature*" (2 Peter 1:4). What a promise that is! The promise of *sharing* in God's nature is greater than the curse of Eden. It means we are not simply stuck with our old natures because we can share in His! Because of Christ, the sinful *dog* inside you loses its bark and its bite.

Throughout the Bible, God tells us that there is hope beyond Eden. The *dog days* are over because of His love for us. We do not have to live a twisted existence that always leads us back to our lesser selves. We have been redeemed. Eden's blood may flow in our veins, but we have been given a transfusion through Christ. (See Ephesians 1:7.) Because of Jesus, we can now share in God's *divine nature.*

This is transformative for you, but it is also revolutionary for your relationships. Your nature may have limited your capacity to love, but Christ in you can free you to experience and share boundless love. You may be broken, but He can use that brokenness to help others. He can move you past your nature and teach you how to have genuine connection with others. You may have a trail of failed relationships, but Jesus can break that pattern. You may be infected by Eden, but Christ is the cure.

~~~~~~~~~~

WE HAVE BEEN REDEEMED. EDEN'S BLOOD MAY FLOW IN OUR VEINS, BUT WE HAVE BEEN GIVEN A TRANSFUSION THROUGH CHRIST.

~~~~~~~~~~

SIN POISONED THE PLAN

Whatever God creates, Satan imitates. In Eden, God created relational perfection. The intimacy and loving relationship we long to have with each other is something God conceived. It was His intention that unending fellowship with Him and lasting relationships with each other would co-exist in perfect harmony. There was never supposed to be a conflict between His holiness and our desires. But sin poisoned the plan. When sin invaded the purity of Eden, it opened the door to imitations. Sin always tries to offer a counterfeit of what we really need. Ever since Eden, mankind has been trying to replace God's intended purity with unreliable pleasures and cheap connections that take the place of real intimacy. Because of the fall, we now have a purity problem. Lust is trying to replace what we lost. And Satan's imitation is not working, although he keeps trying.

Today, when it comes to sexuality, the primary cultural lie is that *ultimate sex* will lead to *ultimate intimacy*. Culture says the connection you desire is found by following the path of your pleasures. This lie may seem modern, but it's not. Deception in the area of sexuality has always been the enemy's go-to weapon. In fact, it may be the most deceptive and destructive lie that he has ever told. For a lie to be truly effective, it must contain elements of the truth. The best lies offer you what you *want* and tell you they have what you *need*. Jesus called the devil *"the father of lies"* (John 8:44). He is an expert at crafting lies that are easy to believe. His lies find their effectiveness in the realm of your hidden desires. When he promises what your heart longs for, it seems like the answer you have been waiting for.

What have you determined about your sexuality? Can it be trusted? Is it affirmed by what Scripture teaches? This area deserves our full attention and our deepest contemplation. There is no stronger temporary relief to your brokenness than sexual sin. It does create an intimate connection, but the wrong kind. Sin always overpromises and under-delivers.

God wants more than a temporary facade of fleeting intimacy for you. He wants your identity to be centered in who He always intended you to be. His identity for your sexuality will create peace in you and end your restless search. Your Father longs to reveal His relational plan to you. Run to Him and run to His Word. The same one who forgives your sin is the one who can show you who you really are.

SEXUAL BROKENNESS

Some time ago, I counseled a married couple who were on the brink of divorce. They no longer felt intimacy; instead, they hated each other. Strangely enough, they confessed to me that they had tried every form of sexual gratification, including inviting other people into their bedroom. I stopped them before they could get too graphic with their confessions, but they kept wanting to elaborate. They had done it all.

SEXUAL SIN PROMISES INTIMACY—BUT IT DESTROYS IT. YOU KNOW THAT SOMETHING IS NOT PART OF GOD'S PLAN IF IT LEAVES YOU *BROKEN* RATHER THAN *BETTER*.

I could not help but think about how they had bought into the great lie. The ultimate sex did not create an ultimate connection. They had been sold a bill of goods. Sexual sin promises intimacy—but it destroys it. Sexual sin always leaves us broken. You know that something is not part of God's plan if it leaves you *broken* rather than *better*.

Paul pleaded, *"Flee from sexual immorality. All other sins a person commits are outside the body, but whoever sins sexually, sins against their own body"* (1 Corinthians 6:18 NIV). This is the only sin for which the Bible makes this distinction: *"sins against their own body."* Paul is saying that all sin has consequences, but sexual sin has an extra layer.

There's a unique problem associated with sex outside of God's original intent: *damage to ourselves.* I have experienced this truth in my distant past and I have prayed with many people who can attest to the self-wounds caused by sexual sin. It makes our broken condition even worse. Keep in mind, sex is never just *skin on skin*; it always involves the intermingling of souls, spirits, hearts, and minds. The experience is deeper than we might care to admit and the damage is far more severe than we realize.

I have prayed with hundreds of people who have found themselves in a state of sexual brokenness. They needed the forgiveness of Jesus, yes, but they also needed something more. So I've learned to pray restorative prayers for the deep damage caused by sexual sin. I always lead sexually broken people in a prayer for God to restore what has been lost or destroyed.

NO MATTER HOW MANY PIECES OF YOURSELF THAT YOU HAVE GIVEN AWAY, THERE IS WHOLENESS WAITING FOR YOU. JESUS KNOWS HOW TO HEAL YOU AND RESTORE WHAT HAS BEEN LOST.

I once counseled a girl at a youth camp who had lost her virginity to a boy she barely knew. She had prayed for forgiveness hundreds of times, but she just could not get back to a place where she felt whole. After two years, she was still filled with guilt and despair. I knew God wanted to renew her. At a church altar, surrounded by hundreds of people, we prayed for restoration—and I watched God restore the light in her eyes and transform her very countenance. It was as if Jesus came down from heaven and healed her from the inside out. She kept saying to me, "It's back! It's back! I can feel God in my life again—it's back!"

Our God is a God of forgiveness and He also is a God of restoration.

No matter how many pieces of yourself that you have given away, there is wholeness waiting for you. Jesus is the *surgeon of heaven* and He knows how to heal you and restore what has been lost. David's plea in Psalm 51 is a great prayer to help restore us from sexual brokenness. David had committed sexual sin and was now destroyed from the inside out. So he prays for both forgiveness and restoration. He asks God to restore *"the joy of your salvation and grant me a willing spirit"* (Psalm 51:12 NIV). God is a restorer. Why wait? If you are sexually broken, pray and ask God to restore you this very moment.

STOLEN PIECES OF INNOCENCE

It was almost 2 a.m. when she sat down next to me. I had been speaking twice a day at a packed event and God was healing lives. For some reason, He was especially dealing with the area of wholeness and healing from sexual sin. The prayer times after the night services kept getting longer as the layers of needs were uncovered. Then I met her. After sitting down, this young girl looked at me and bluntly asked, "Where was God when I was raped?" She gave me some details and it was worse than you can imagine. I don't know where my response came from, but I blurted out, "He was right in the room when it happened and He is here tonight." I immediately regretted saying that, but I knew I had been prompted by God. As you can imagine, the girl became enraged.

"If He was there, then why didn't He stop it?" she said. "I hate God."

My training had not prepared me for that moment. All I knew to do was to be authentic and let the wisdom and the love of God flow through me.

"That is a choice you can make—you can choose to hate God," I told her. "I am not here to defend Him and I have no idea why He did not stop this from happening. If you choose to be bitter, then you will always be able to use this tragedy as an excuse for anything that goes wrong in your life."

I let her know that justifiable bitterness—when we have every reason to feel anger, hurt, and sorrow—can be like a warm blanket that covers all our faults and failures. But every bitterness comes with a price. "The price of a bitter life," I told this girl, "is that it is all about you. A bitter life is a life that does not help others."

So I challenged her to let God bring purpose out of her pain. To my shock, she agreed. I was so proud to see her pray deep prayers of forgiveness for her abuser and restoration for herself. She was not setting *him* free; she was setting *herself* free. She walked away that night determined to let God use her story.

If she can do that, so can we.

To get back to Eden, we must deal with what we have given away, but we also must address what has been stolen. Maybe you are among the millions who have been sexually abused or raped. Your innocence was stolen from you. For many, this happens at an age when they are unable to defend themselves. Unfortunately, even people who are supposed to be our protectors can be predators. Nothing is more evil than that. What do you do with that kind of betrayal? How do you even process that level of pain? I would never say I have all the answers, but I do have an idea: perhaps one of the reasons God wants to heal you is so that you can help others. He can bring purpose out of your pain.

The road back to Eden is not an easy one. Jesus once described the way to life as a narrow gateway and a road that few find, while the highway to hell is wide and many take it. (See Matthew 7:13–14.) The road of a pleasure-seeking, bitter life is wide and crowded. The way of restoration is narrow and rare. But the longings of your soul are pulling you away from the masses. God is beckoning you into a beautiful wilderness filled with the relational health He intends you to have. There is forgiveness, wholeness, and healing. There is a better way.

WORTH FIGHTING FOR

Years ago, I read about a man who got his car stuck in a snowbank. He tried and tried, but he couldn't get it out. He became so enraged that he took out his tire iron and smashed all the windows. Then he pulled a shotgun out of his trunk and shot all four tires. That wasn't enough for him, so he reloaded and fired several shots into his engine. Someone called the police, but there was no crime because this *vehicular homicide* was committed against his own car. What a waste! All that energy and ammunition spent to destroy something of value. All that rage directed at something that had nothing to do with his destiny.

There is so much rage in the world today. Road rage. Workplace rage. Rage over politics and religion. Rage about all the rights we are supposed to have.

Anger is everywhere. It has certainly found its way into our relationships. A lot of us feel like we're stuck in the snowbanks of our lives. So we struggle and lash out; we become enraged and waste our energy on behaviors that won't fix the problem. Why? Why do we put our deepest emotions into things that are unproductive and unworthy? It's like we are swinging at everything, just hoping to hit something. All we end up doing is destroying things of value and ourselves in the process.

Nothing destroys relationships like misplaced rage. It can be demonstrative and loud, like beating up a car in a snowbank, or it can be deadly silent. Our anger can calmly exist beneath the surface, where it seeps into our personalities and steals our ability to meaningfully connect with others.

What is the source of all this negative energy? I believe it flows from the *acceptance of less*. We have been made for *more*, but we have accepted *less*.

I recently saw a television special that revealed a sneaky form of inflation. Our favorite products are giving us *less* for the same price as the *more* we once had. The new concaved bottom on peanut butter jars is stealing away a full ounce of spreadable goodness. Cereal boxes are thinner. Ice cream is no longer sold by the gallon. We are paying more, but are getting less—and we have done nothing to stop it.

One less peanut butter sandwich is not a tragedy, but a less-full life is. Our souls know what they have been created for. When we are constantly presented with lesser versions, counterfeits of what should be, our souls are aware of the concession. That *dream job* did not fulfill you after all and that new thing *you just had to have* was not worth what you paid. The experience you fantasized about fell short of expectations. Your *Stacy* checked the *yes* box, but the relationship is not what you thought it would be.

WHEN WE ARE CONSTANTLY PRESENTED
WITH LESSER VERSIONS,
COUNTERFEITS OF WHAT SHOULD BE,
OUR SOULS ARE AWARE OF THE CONCESSION.

Relationships are probably the area where most people feel cheated. After a while, we feel we have no choice but to accept something less than what we need. You know at the soul level that you are not fulfilled, but what can you do about it? A river of rage begins to flow.

Anger takes a lot of energy. Many people carry a tiredness caused by anger from unresolved conflict. What if we could direct the resources of our hearts and minds toward a solution to the problem? Instead of silently seething over the *less* that this world offers, what if we fought for the *more* God wants us to have? These words of the apostle Paul can help to get you into a mind-set for that battle:

> *Think about the things of heaven, not the things of earth. For you died to this life, and your real life is hidden with Christ in God.*
>
> (Colossians 3:2–3)

When we move the focus of our minds away from the lesser things of this earth and toward the greater things of heaven, something tremendous happens. We start searching for the *life* that is *"hidden with Christ in God."* Instead of accepting less, we fight for much, much more.

I remember talking to a young man a few years ago who was making tragic decisions in the area of relationships. He was pursuing a sexual lifestyle that was far from what God desired for him. I told him that he was willingly allowing his relational future to be sacrificed on the altar of what he thought he wanted. God was giving me a vision of the wife he was supposed to marry and the children he was supposed to have. I told him, "Your future family is worth fighting for." He was settling for less because *less* was something he could have right away. *More* always takes longer to become a reality—but it's worth the wait and the fight. That day, the young man chose his better relational future. We need to do likewise.

If you spend the rest of your days pursuing God and what He has for you, your life will be well spent. Most people settle for far less than what God intends for them to have. *You* are not most people. Most people never dream about Eden—but *you* do. Most people never acknowledge that their soul is longing for something it was born to have—like *you* do. By virtue of simply reading this chapter, you are now aware that God has something *better* for you, something *more*. The answer to your *aloneness* is found in the One who created you for *more*. The relationships God has for you will be birthed out of the work He is doing in you. What could be better than that? What deserves your energy more? This is a life worth fighting for.

DISCOVERY QUESTIONS

Why do our souls still long for Eden?

_____

_____

_____

_____

What made Adam and Eve naked but unashamed?

_____

_____

_____

_____

Why did God place the tree of knowledge in the garden?

_____

_____

_____

_____

How is shame worse than guilt?

_____

_____

_____

_____

SIX

THE FORGIVENESS FACTOR

Forgive one another as quickly and thoroughly as
God in Christ forgave you.
—Ephesians 4:32 (MSG)

One of my greatest memories of forgiveness is also one of my favorite moments with my dad. He does not remember it as well as I do, but the events of that day impacted me in ways I will never forget. It was the summer after my freshman year of Bible college. I had one year of ministry study under my belt, but I still had a lot of growing to do. I came home with a desire to hang out with old friends and make some memories before heading back to school. It took me a while to reconnect, but one morning, the phone rang with an invitation.

My friends and I were wannabe outdoorsmen. We liked fishing and hunting, but the latter was more along the lines of *shooting some stuff*. My buddies were heading into the fields and invited me to tag along. Without thinking, I jumped at the chance to blow off work and have fun.

I went into my room to get my .22 rifle and my single-shot, 20-gauge shotgun out from under my bed, but then I had a thought—a dumb, selfish thought driven by my immaturity and an insecure desire to be liked. I thought, *These guns are old and unimpressive. I should take something different. I should take Dad's shotgun, his nice 12-gauge automatic.* I knew Dad would not lend the gun to me just so I could shoot some stuff with my buddies, but my idea was to *borrow* it without permission, clean it, and return it before he knew what happened. My idea worked like a charm…for a while. My friends were impressed and I was shooting like a champ. I love it when a plan comes together, even a bad one.

But then, something happened. Somewhere in our reckless travels through those fields, I must have tripped and got some mud in the end of the barrel. The next time I shot, the barrel exploded and mushroomed back on itself. Thank God no one was hurt, but my dad's prized gun was destroyed. It was like a mishap from an old Elmer Fudd cartoon. Both the event and its impact on me seemed to happen in slow motion. I stared at the gun in disbelief as the bitter reality of what happened washed over me. My friends rolled on the ground with uncontrollable laughter. The gun I lied about and bragged about was now a mangled mess. I reacted by yelling. "Stop laughing! This is not my gun! I am in so much trouble…"

THE WORST GUILT TRIP

Then came the long car ride home. I could no longer fit the gun in the trunk, so it sat in the front passenger seat next to me, mocking me all the way home. Every one of us has probably had a *trip home* like the one I had that day. It seemed like the car slowly drove itself while my mind raced, thinking about what I had done. I was preparing for ministry, yet I had broken my dad's trust and destroyed something he loved. I had been so stupid and deceitful. I wish I could say that guilt was utmost in my mind, but I was mostly concerned with my self-preservation. My parents were sacrificing to send me to college and now I had done *this*. I was supposed to be the *good kid* in the family! *What would everyone think when they found out what I had done? Would my parents even continue their support? Would they ever trust me again? What is Dad going to do to me?* In my mind, my life was basically over.

Before I knew it, I was back in our driveway. My dad's truck was parked in front of me. He had just arrived home from work. I stared at that truck and contemplated my fate. I only had a couple of choices: go inside and confess my crime, which would end my existence as I had known it; or leave home and become a homeless teenager. I seriously contemplated the latter.

After a long pause, I reluctantly grabbed the mangled gun and walked up the driveway. I tried to hide it behind my back as I walked into the house. Dad looked at me. "What's that?"

I leaned what was left of his prized possession against the counter. Like it, I was fully exposed and had no defense. I explained what had happened and then quickly shut my mouth.

I stood there waiting for the fireworks to start. But instead of freaking out, Dad was quiet. Deathly silent. I thought that was a bad sign. About two minutes went by, but it felt like hours. Finally, Dad broke the silence. Speaking in a calm, low tone, he said, "Son, you have done some stupid things in your life and this is definitely one of them."

I gave a shaky reply. "Yes, sir."

Then he said, "But…"

But? I was not expecting to hear that hope-filled, three-letter word.

"YOU ARE FORGIVEN"

Dad said, "But a while back, I went to church with you and your mom and received Christ and He forgave me." Since he was mentioning church, I thought surely he was about to point out the obvious hypocrisy of this *preacher-in-training* son of his, the very same son who had invited him to church. But he did nothing of the sort. Instead he said, "So I think I owe you this one. You are forgiven. Now, what would you like for supper?"

Just like that. I could not believe what I was hearing. *How could this be? What was he trying to pull?* I was stunned. All I could think was, *This cannot be real.* I rapidly questioned the sincerity of this *forgiveness* he spoke of. I even begged him for a punishment and foolishly offered several suggestions of what he should do to me. Several times, I actually tried to talk him out of the grace he was offering. I promised to work for money to buy a new gun, which for a poor college student is more of a fantasy than a promise. Dad just became firmer in his resolve to forgive me.

He finally stopped me in mid-sentence. "Son, you can't pay for this one. You are forgiven. Now, what would you like for supper?"

I replied with an emotion-filled thank-you and offered a dinner suggestion. I cautiously walked past Dad and headed into my room to contemplate what had just happened. I was forgiven, but I wore it like a life jacket that was too big for me. I was uncomfortable with what had happened, but I had no choice. I had to accept it. I was forgiven.

It would be years before I began to contemplate the depth of this event. You see, Dad forgave me because he had been forgiven. Dad gave me the very gift he himself had received. Nothing is more like Jesus than that. I had helped to bring him to Christ, but I had violated his deep trust and made him a victim of my undeveloped character. Instead of calling out my inconsistency, he remembered his own moment of forgiveness. Dad gave me mercy when I deserved judgment. Grace like that changes both the giver and the recipient. I have still not recovered from it.

This true story happened more than thirty years ago, yet it impacts my thoughts and emotions to this day. Dad's forgiveness affected me at a soul-level. Forgiveness done right has a restorative quality to it. The worse the offense, the greater the forgiveness and the deeper the impact. I believe I'm a better forgiver today because of what Dad modeled for me. That event caused me to parent more gracefully and teach the principles of forgiveness more often. The emotional dynamics of that day originated with a spiritual event. Dad's own experience with grace helped him to give grace. When you are overwhelmed with the reality of being forgiven, it naturally and supernaturally overflows from you. Forgiveness creates forgivers.

WHEN YOU ARE OVERWHELMED WITH THE REALITY OF BEING FORGIVEN, IT NATURALLY AND SUPERNATURALLY OVERFLOWS FROM YOU. FORGIVENESS CREATES FORGIVERS.

Although he may not have fully contemplated it, Dad practiced this divine principle when he forgave me. I believe my father modeled this verse from Paul that day: *"Forgive one another as quickly and thoroughly as God in Christ forgave you"* (Ephesians 4:32 MSG). Dad forgave quickly and thoroughly, just as Christ had forgiven him.

YOUR BEST *GRACE MOMENTS* ARE EMPOWERED BY THE GRACE YOU RECEIVE IN YOUR WORST MOMENTS.

You function in grace better when you remember that *you* have been forgiven. Your best *grace moments* are empowered by the grace you receive in your worst moments. The problem is, most of us fail to make the connection. Most grace is only received grace; it never graduates to grace given. This is both tragic and wasteful because grace is meant to be passed on. Grace never completes its assigned journey until it is both received and given away. Forgiven people forgive people.

We all have been hurt like I hurt my dad that day. Maybe someone stole something from you and destroyed it. Maybe you were betrayed by someone you loved and trusted. You have probably been hurt by someone you poured your life into. Part of the broken system of this fallen world is our tendency to wound each other. Sometimes it's a reaction caused by our endless insecurities; sometimes it's just a choice that flows from the evil in our hearts. The pain never seems to end. The victimizations we experience come equally from *outsiders* and those who are on the *inside* of our own relational worlds. In fact, proximity makes it easier for someone to hurt you. Family and friends often have the clearest shots at our hearts. Many have also been hurt by the church. Most of us are riddled with scars from past betrayals. The need for forgiveness has never been greater than it is today.

Since you have read this far, I'm going to assume two things about you. First, you know what it is to be hurt. Second, you know what it is to be forgiven. What I hope to do is to take those two facts and create a spiritual combination that will open the door to a divine conclusion: *the fact that someone hurts you must be filtered through the fact that you have been forgiven.* You may be the offended one today, but yesterday, you were the offender. How can you want unlimited grace for yourself and then be stingy when giving out grace to others? Freely you received, now freely you must give. The ultimate celebration of what God has done for you is to do the same for someone else. You are never more like your Savior than when you forgive. And there is healing in the act of forgiving. Your restoration is not complete until you forgive those who wounded you.

JESUS MAKES THE MATH GO CRAZY

Math was not my favorite subject in school. Some people take comfort in the cold truth of numbers, but I always found them to be a bit harsh. Adding up the cost of something is not nearly as fun as just dreaming about having it! But we need numbers because they never lie. Jesus once used this fact to make a powerful point about forgiveness. In Matthew 18, Jesus is again teaching through parables, the *truth bombs* of Scripture. These stories from God have far-reaching applications.

After teaching His disciples what to do if a brother or sister in the church sins, Peter asks Jesus, *"Lord, how often should I forgive someone who sins against me? Seven times?"* (Matthew 18:21). Why does he ask this? Maybe Peter has been hurt by someone who claimed to follow Jesus. His question is interesting because he turns forgiveness into a mathematical equation. Peter probably feels like he is being generous by offering to forgive someone seven times.

Then Jesus causes the math to go crazy. *"No, not seven times,"* Jesus replied, *"but seventy times seven!"* (Matthew 18:22). Jesus pushes the forgiveness quotient to an exhausting 490 times. I can only imagine what Peter must have been feeling! I think we *might* be able to handle seven offenses from someone if we are feeling gracious, but 490? That seems abusive and impossible. But Jesus is saying, "Stop trying to count offenses and stop measuring forgiveness." I don't believe He was giving us a baseline number of how many times we must show grace. Instead, Jesus was telling us that forgiveness is a never-ending circle of receiving and giving grace. We breathe in His forgiveness and we breathe out forgiveness to others. Forgiveness is a lifestyle, not an event.

WE BREATHE IN HIS FORGIVENESS AND WE
BREATHE OUT FORGIVENESS TO OTHERS.
FORGIVENESS IS A LIFESTYLE, NOT AN EVENT.

In my own life, I have discovered that sometimes, I must forgive over and over again to get past an offense. If you have been hurt deeply, you may have to forgive daily. It may take weeks or even months for your mind and emotions to catch up with your intentional choice to forgive. We must forgive, even if it takes us 490 times—or more. Eventually, the mental scenarios of revenge will come to an end. The urge toward self-preservation will fade. *Payback* will be replaced by *pay it forward*.

When it comes to God's grace, trust the process. You will be restored when you refuse to take revenge. God is your protector and your justice; you do not have to be in charge. Mercy will ultimately triumph over judgment. (See James 2:13.) Embrace your Savior's math and become an endless forgiver.

Before Peter has a chance to crunch the numbers, Jesus jumps right in with a story about a king who wanted to settle the accounts of his servants. (See Matthew 18:23–34.) One servant owes an astronomical amount—*"millions of dollars," "ten thousand bags of gold"* (NIV), or *"ten thousand talents"* (NKJV). Think "gross national debt" kind of money! This was a sum so large that he could never pay it back; some translators say it was *at least* twenty years' wages. So the king ordered that this servant, his family, and all of their possessions be sold so he could recoup some of his money.

Then this indebted servant begs for mercy—and his master showed great compassion, forgiving the entire debt, a debt much larger than the man could ever repay. Can you imagine that? This would be a life-altering event of mercy for anyone. To be forgiven like that would, or should, change you forever.

You would think that the rest of the story would be about the servant's gratitude, but instead, Jesus takes us on an unexpected journey about the abuse of grace. This *forgiven servant* walks out of the king's presence and runs into a fellow servant who owed him about a day's wages, a small amount compared to what *he* had owed the king. So, he shows mercy, right? He forgives like he has just been forgiven, right? I wish that *was* the story. He grabs the other servant by the throat and says, *"Pay back what you owe me!"* (Matthew 18:28 NIV). Then he throws the poor guy into prison until the small debt can be paid. (See Matthew 18:30.)

This is hypocrisy at the highest level. The *forgiven servant* has spiritual amnesia. How could he not relate the forgiveness he *received* to the forgiveness he should now *give*? He is completely ignoring the spiritual mathematics. Unfortunately for him, some other servants witnessed the whole thing and were outraged, so they went to the king and told him what happened. (See Matthew 18:31.) Understandably, the king is enraged, reverses his decision, and throws the servant into prison, where he's to be tortured until the entire debt is repaid. (See Matthew 18:32–34.)

The last verse of this parable is one of the scariest in the Bible. Jesus tells His disciples, *"That's what my heavenly Father will do to you if you refuse to forgive your brothers and sisters from your heart"* (Matthew 18:35). I hope Jesus is exaggerating here, or we might be in trouble. Jesus *is* saying that a lack of forgiveness prompts judgment in the heart of God. God expects us to forgive as we have been forgiven.

The hypocrisy of this story is staggering, but it can be calculated. The second servant owed the forgiven man just one day's wages, whereas he owed at least twenty years' wages to the king—or 7,300 days' worth. Yet he refuses to forgive! Jesus is telling us that God will always make the *math* work out in our favor, if we will forgive.

In this parable, you and I are the servant who has been forgiven. The sum amount of my sin was so large that it created a debt that I could never reconcile. I deserved judgment, but my master gave me forgiveness.

Like the unforgiving servant, I often suffer from *spiritual amnesia*. I fail to make the connection between what I have been given and what I should give to others. My math is off and so is yours. We are the forgiven who need to learn how to forgive.

OUR CALCULATORS ARE BROKEN

Many years ago, Jeanne and I went to dinner with a large group of old friends from my hometown. When I was out of earshot, one of the ladies began to apologize to Jeanne for treating me poorly in the past. She was speaking on behalf of a combination of people who had often treated me disrespectfully. She saw what God was doing with my life and was embarrassed that they had not shown more confidence in me.

Later that night, we stopped at a store and Jeanne told me about this conversation. I was happy to hear about both the apology and my wife's gracious response. Rare moments like that require special attention.

Then Jeanne asked me a question that she has often posed to me. She's noticed this group of friends treat me poorly over the years and wondered, "Why have you never fought back or defended yourself?" Instead of answering right away, I asked her to give me a minute while I went into the store to get our drinks. I had to think about it.

When I returned, my beautiful wife looked at me expectantly.

"Honey, I guess I decided a long time ago that I would let God defend me," I told her. "I decided that *I would not do the math*. I knew what they were doing. *I knew that two plus two is supposed to equal four.* I knew that their disrespectful behavior meant something. But I decided that God would be in charge and keep track *of the score of their offenses*. It's His right to *do the math—I refuse to finish the equation. My spiritual calculator belongs to Him."*

Jeanne is used to me speaking in illustrations. The Holy Spirit was in the car with us and He brought about a full understanding. Jeanne was so patient as we talked about not being offended, not even on behalf of each other. We talked about how God could keep track of our offenses so we didn't have to. We talked about how the miracle of the apology that night would have never happened if I supervised my own defense. We made a commitment to let God be in charge of *the math* when it relates to how others treat us. We both decided that we would always surrender our *calculators* over to Him. We will think the best and let God deal with the motives of people's hearts. We will let God be our defender and our avenger.

Our relationships with God and each other reached new heights that night. Forgiveness is liberating. Forgiveness sets both you and your offenders free—in that order.

FORGIVENESS IS LIBERATING.
FORGIVENESS SETS BOTH YOU AND YOUR
OFFENDERS FREE—IN THAT ORDER.

I already told you that math is not one of my strengths. This is especially true when it comes to *doing the math* on the intentions and motives of others. Suppose a person walks by you in the hallway at work and doesn't even look at you, much less say hello. You quickly engage your *mental calculator* and before you know it, you have *completed the math*. Two plus two equals they must hate me! Someone hurts you and you think you know their motivation and intent. Most of the time, however, you're wrong. Your *calculator* is broken. Only God has access to people's minds and hearts. And for the few times you get the math right, you're not doing yourself or the other person any good. You are supposed to love, think the best, and forgive. You are even supposed to love and forgive your enemies. Even when you get the math right, you're still wrong. Forgiveness is always right and unforgiveness is always wrong. You won't learn *that* from a calculator.

What if we permanently put Jesus in charge of the math? What if we let Him be Lord over our conclusions? He would be our freedom and our defender, for He always gets the *math* right. *"The* LORD *detests the use of dishonest scales, but he delights in accurate weights"* (Proverbs 11:1). The Lord hates it when we get the math wrong. The way to have *"accurate weights"* in your life is to love others as God loves you. When you live like that, God will always tip the scales in your favor.

~~~

FORGIVENESS IS NOT ABOUT LETTING SOMEONE GET AWAY WITH WHAT THEY HAVE DONE; IT'S ABOUT TRANSFERRING THE RESPONSIBILITY FOR DEALING WITH WHAT HAPPENED TO GOD.

~~~

God's *calculator* has a *judgment key.* Forgiveness is not about letting someone get away with what they have done; it's about transferring the responsibility for dealing with what happened to God. He is the only one who can truly administer justice. In his letter to the church in Rome, Paul wrote, *"Do not take revenge, my dear friends, but leave room for God's wrath, for it is written: 'It is mine to avenge; I will repay,' says the Lord"* (Romans 12:19 NIV). Notice the emphatic nature of this verse. God says He *"will repay."* He assures us that what has happened to us will not be ignored.

If only we would *"leave room for God's wrath."* Most of us leave no room for God to move! We say all that we want to say and do all that we can think of doing. We defend ourselves until there is nothing left to defend. But God says excessive self-defense only decreases His ability to move on our behalf. Would you rather fight your own battles, or would you like the God of wisdom and power to fight for you? Lay down your sword and let Him be your warrior. He will win the battle in ways that you never could.

MUCH FORGIVEN = MUCH LOVE

Right now you may be thinking, *This is asking for too much!* I certainly can relate to that sentiment. Forgiveness can be one of the hardest things God asks us to do. *"Forgiving one another, even as God in Christ forgave you"* (Ephesians 4:32 NKJV) will require divine assistance. But there is a special source of power we can all depend on. The strength of the Lord's love for us enables us to forgive. You can't do it on your own, but you can with Christ in you. There is an event that took place during the ministry of Jesus that proves this point.

In Luke 7:36–50, Jesus is invited to dinner at the house of a powerful religious leader named Simon. They have barely sat down to eat when a *sinful woman* crashes the party. This story starts strong and it gets even better.

Many Bible scholars believe this woman must have been a prostitute. Various translations of the story call her *"immoral," "the town harlot,"* and an *"especially wicked sinner."* We also know from this encounter that Jesus had already met this woman and forgiven her life of sin. Somehow, she discovers where Jesus is going to have dinner and her forgiven heart is drawn there. The joyful fragrance of grace entices her to the home of Simon, where Jesus is dining. Maybe she doesn't understand the jeopardy she will be in by ignoring the social and religious protocol of her day. Maybe she just doesn't care. She could suffer rejection and humiliation, but she *has* to see Jesus. Seemingly oblivious to the norms of her time, she runs through the mental hurdles and walks right into the house where Jesus is sitting. She is now only a few feet from her Savior. Simon is dazed. Jesus is delighted.

This forgiven sinner falls in front of Jesus and does something beautiful. She begins washing His feet with her many tears. People are staring in judgment, but overwhelming gratitude is spilling out of her. She holds nothing back as she kisses the feet of the one who set her free. She even opens an expensive jar of perfume and puts it all over the tear-soaked feet of Jesus. She wipes off the excess with her long hair. Simon is appalled and says to himself, *"If this man were a prophet, he would know what kind of woman is touching him. She's a sinner!"* (Luke 7:39).

Jesus reads Simon's mind and answers his mental disdain with a story. He tells Simon about a money lender who forgives two debts, one much higher than the other. Then Jesus asks the obvious question, *"Who do you suppose loved him more after that?"* (Luke 7:42). Simon's answer unintentionally highlights a powerful principle: *"I suppose the one for whom he canceled the larger debt"* (Luke 7:43). The one who is forgiven more loves more. Indeed, this woman *does* love Jesus more.

Jesus points out that Simon neglected the most basic hospitality customs of their day. (See Luke 7:44–46.) He provided no water or towel for Jesus to wash his feet. Simon offered no kiss as he greeted the Savior of the world, nor did he anoint His head with oil. But this forgiven woman washed Jesus's feet with her tears, dried them with her hair, kissed them with unquenchable gratitude, and anointed Jesus with perfume. Then Jesus shows Simon where the power to love and forgive comes from. *"I tell you, her sins—and they are many—have been forgiven, so she has shown me much love. But a person who is forgiven little shows only little love"* (Luke 7:47).

Little forgiveness produces little love. Great forgiveness enlarges our capacity to love.

WHEN WE STRUGGLE TO LOVE,
IT'S BECAUSE WE FAIL TO CORRELATE THE LOVE
RECEIVED WITH LOVE THAT MUST BE *GIVEN*.
EVERY FORGIVEN PERSON IS GIVEN THE MANDATE
AND THE POWER TO FORGIVE.

If you are a Christ follower, then you have been forgiven much. When we struggle to love, it's because we fail to correlate the love *received* with love that must be *given*. Every forgiven person is given both the mandate and the power to forgive. If this sinful woman in Luke 7 can invade a dinner party to express gratitude to Jesus, then we must follow her example. It's time to *intentionally live* from the fact that you are loved. Nothing will empower your ability to love and forgive more than celebrating the fact that you are perfectly and deeply loved by God.

Think of Christ's love and forgiveness like a new river being established in the desert. The land was dry and barren before the river was released. Now, everywhere you look, there is life. Previously, you struggled to survive; now, you can thrive. Once, you had to measure out anything you gave away because there was so little; now, there's a surplus for everyone.

When you are loved and forgiven by Jesus, it establishes a mighty river in the desert places of your soul. Out of the abundance of what you have been given, you can now bless others. You have been given much, now you can love much. Grace creates an overflow.

BOOMERANG BULLETS

I've never been in a shootout, but I've watched plenty of them on TV. That's right—I am a bit of an armchair expert when it comes to gun battles. You name it: westerns, sci-fi, war movies, or cop shows, I have seen them all. From what I can tell, people shoot at other people for a wide variety of reasons. They want to protect themselves or others, they're angry or afraid—or a combination of these factors.

We *fire away* for the same reasons when people hurt us. Pain eventually expresses itself. Unresolved hurt leads to bitterness, and bitter people are inclined to wage war with everyone and everything around them. Bitter people use a lot of ammunition. Life has handed them lemons and instead of making lemonade, they use them for target practice.

In my ministry, I have met a lot of *bitter shooters*. Their mouths become *verbal guns* loaded with the combustible frustration that comes from being victimized by life. They're masters of the *preemptive strike* because, sure as shootin', *no one* is going to hurt them again. No, sir, they are nobody's fool. They are suspicious of every relationship.

Bitter people self-sabotage themselves by filtering every interaction through the lens of their hurt. Their future is stalled because of the constant mental repetition of a painful past. Like quick-draw gunslingers, anyone and anything can be in their sights at a moment's notice. Bitterness is always ready for a fight.

When counseling someone who is bitter, it can be difficult to get past the layers of hurt, anger, and pride. But I have found that almost everyone wants to be better. Our souls instinctively know that bitterness is poison. In our hearts, we know that the anger that is supposedly protecting us is actually killing us.

OUR SOULS INSTINCTIVELY KNOW THAT BITTERNESS IS POISON. IN OUR HEARTS, WE KNOW THAT THE ANGER THAT IS SUPPOSEDLY PROTECTING US IS ACTUALLY KILLING US.

Everyone who is bitter is also conflicted. The hurting heart is speaking to the enraged mind and pleading for mercy. God has a way of opening us up when we are suffering and helping us to seek honest counsel. In rare moments like that, I always talk about what I call the *boomerang effect*.

When you load your mind with bitter thoughts and shoot out bitter words, your intention is to hurt the people who hurt you...or at least get someone else to understand what they did to you. But *bitter bullets* always return home—the *boomerang effect*. What is meant for others ends up hurting ourselves the most. When you speak words of bitterness over another person, you are really speaking them over yourself. Solomon wrote, *"A soothing tongue [speaking words that build up and encourage] is a tree of life, but a perversive tongue [speaking words that overwhelm and depress] crushes the spirit"* (Proverbs 15:4 AMP). Another translation tells us that a perverse tongue *"breaks the spirit"* (NKJV).

You can speak healing over yourself and others, or your words can break you down. Expressed bitterness opens you up to a world of inner turmoil. *Bitter bullets boomerang* and penetrate the protective layers of your own soul.

Proverbs also tell us, *"A sound mind makes for a robust body, but runaway emotions corrode the bones"* (Proverbs 14:30 MSG). I am no medical expert, but I have witnessed the effects of *runaway emotions* on far too many lives. Most of us know from personal experience that our emotional state impacts our physical health. There is an undeniable *boomerang effect* for those who choose bitterness and unforgiveness. It makes us feel bad, creates stress, and leads to depression. Bitterness lessens our capacity to be healthy; it isolates us so it can destroy us. When are we going to learn? Forgiveness is the best medicine. Bitterness is just not worth it.

YOUR SPIRITUAL GPS

James compared our tongues to the bit in a horse's mouth or a ship's rudder. (See James 3:2–4.) Your words are the guidance system of your life and your tongue is your personal GPS system. How you talk determines where you ultimately end up. This is a real problem for someone who chooses to live a life of unforgiveness because our words flow from our thoughts and feelings. You do not have to be around a bitter person for very long before you hear bitter language.

Jesus said, *"Out of the abundance of the heart the mouth speaks"* (Matthew 12:34 NKJV). What's inside you will come out of you. And according to James, what is coming out of you will end up directing you. When you speak bitter words, you end up walking down bitter roads. You end up in bitter places. Bitterness never leads us anyplace that God intended us to go.

WHEN YOU SPEAK BITTER WORDS,
YOU END UP WALKING DOWN BITTER ROADS.
BITTERNESS NEVER LEADS US ANYPLACE THAT
GOD INTENDED US TO GO.

The writer of Hebrews exhorts us, *"Work at living in peace with everyone, and work at living a holy life.… Watch out that no poisonous **root of bitterness** grows up to trouble you, **corrupting many**"* (Hebrews 12:14–15).

When you choose bitterness, a *root system* begins to extend outward from you, looking for anything it can draw life from. It will corrupt your family and destroy all of your relationships. Bitter people never walk bitter roads alone; they always have *unwilling stowaways* taking the unhealthy journey with them.

The road that leads to the life you are meant to have is not a smooth road. It's filled with *potholes of pain* and *speed bumps of betrayal*. How you handle these obstacles will not only determine where you are going, but also *who you are* when you get there. Forgiveness makes us more like Jesus; bitterness makes us more like the enemy. Forgiveness and bitterness are *directional decisions* leading to completely different places. One leads to the life you were meant to have; the other leads you away from it.

I live in Kansas City, so if I want to travel to Denver, I head west. I can travel east and *hope* I get to Denver, but I will only get further away from it. Decisions determine direction. This is both a natural and spiritual law. Where do you want to go? I want to go to every place God intends for me to be. I want every relationship He wants me to have. I want to end up being the person He envisions me to be. Forgiveness leads me to His *divine intentions* and bitterness takes me away from them. I want my spiritual GPS to always be pointed in the direction of *grace*.

DISCOVERY QUESTIONS

Why is it so important to give mercy rather than pass judgment?

_____

_____

_____

_____

_____

How often should you forgive someone who sins against you? Why?

_____

_____

_____

_____

What is the boomerang effect of anger, bitterness, or resentment?

_____

_____

_____

_____

How has your tongue acted like "a ship's rudder" in your life?

_____

_____

_____

_____

PART III:

RELABELED

SEVEN

STICKY BUSINESS

Once you label me, you negate me.
—Søren Kierkegaard

Things became blurry when I was in second grade. I had been squinting to see the chalkboard for quite some time. Eventually, my teacher told my mom that I should have my vision checked. A few weeks later, I put on my first pair of eyeglasses...about three decades before that was cool. My parents said I *had* to wear them, especially in class, so every weekday morning, I reluctantly put them on and headed off to school to be judged. At that age, I did not have a lot of confidence to begin with. Now I had to wear glasses to help me to see the world better. My real fear was that the world would see me. Up until then, I had successfully avoided anything that would bring attention to myself.

Those glasses might as well have had flashing lights on them. Everybody seemed to notice. A few days after I got them, my glasses and I walked into Webster Elementary and, almost immediately, someone yelled out, "Four eyes!" This childhood insult is my first memory of being *labeled*. That label stuck to the clean canvas of my young mind with an unexpected force. The term quickly took over my thoughts and dominated my unformed identity.

I was emotionally branded and scarred. The words affected me so deeply that I vowed to never let it happen again. So I started doing my own version of Clark Kent…without the Superman part. Every day on the way to school, I would step into a proverbial phone booth and take the glasses off. The guilt of disobeying my parents could not compare with the pain that label caused me. I would rather struggle to see than be seen by those who would harm me.

I am a pretty logical person. I can remember standing in front of my bedroom mirror, looking at my glasses and thinking, *Four eyes! That does not even make sense.* My seven-year-old brain surmised that these glasses make my eyes see better, but they do not add two more eyes! I wish I had had the courage to explain to my attackers how their argument lacked a logical context. I wish I could have straightened my glasses and showed them how their *label* was stupid on multiple levels. But the truth is, my efforts to educate would have failed. Labelers—especially the ones still in grade school—care nothing about logic. Labelers depend on surface judgment and they fail to consider the person behind the label. The Danish theologian Søren Kierkegaard once said, "When you label me, you negate me." To negate is to deny the truth about someone or something. Labelers deny the true value of a person. When you belittle someone this way, you are attempting to nullify them and rob them of their worth.

JUDGMENT BASED ON OUTWARD APPEARANCE
REPRESENTS THE LOWEST PART OF OUR NATURE.
IT GIVES AN EVIL VOICE TO OUR
SINFUL HUMAN CONDITION.

We are never less like God than when we label someone. God never does that. *"The LORD sees not as man sees: man looks on the outward appearance, but the LORD looks on the heart"* (1 Samuel 16:7 ESV). When we judge based on outward appearance, we are representing the lowest part of our nature. This kind of judgment gives an evil voice to our sinful human condition. It reveals more about the one judging than the one being judged—and it causes the latter to retreat into a shell of self-hatred. Labels diminish personal potential while love increases it. Anyone who has worn a new pair of glasses in the second grade knows that.

The truth is, we mostly judge others out of our fear of being judged ourselves. But when we believe in people, when we look at their hearts, we are emulating God Himself. Loving people despite their rough outward layers opens divine possibilities.

WHAT MAKES LABELS STICK

Every one of us has experienced the pain of a label. Someone pointed at you and called out what they thought they saw, mercilessly summing you up with a single word, phrase, or sentence. They delivered their lie like a boxer delivers a punch and it left its mark. It pierced your defenses and penetrated your very identity. It stuck to your psyche like Velcro.

The real question is, why did it work? Why are labels so powerful and painful? What makes them *stick*? How did the person who said, "Sticks and stones may break my bones, but words will never hurt me" avoid the pain of a label? Labels are hard to remove and they always leave a scar. They can even be permanent if we don't deal with them.

A label takes advantage of a person's obvious or hidden insecurities, which make up the *glue* that causes the label to stick. Insecurity is almost as old as time itself, since it originated in the garden of Eden. Adam and Eve *"were both naked, but they felt no shame"* (Genesis 2:25). There was no insecurity. They only knew love, the love of God and the love of each other. The simplicity of their reality left no room for the deceptive complexity of self-doubt.

Then, in Genesis 3, the serpent deceives the couple and they sin. The rest of this passage shows us the entry point of insecurity. *"At that moment their eyes were opened, and they suddenly felt shame at their nakedness. So they sewed fig leaves together to cover themselves"* (Genesis 3:7). Suddenly, the enemy's labels have something to stick to. Sin opens the door and insecurity rushes in. Things become sticky fast.

What happens next is both tragic and enlightening. Adam and Eve hide because of what they have done. God comes looking for them and calls out, "Where are you?" (See Genesis 3:8–9.) Adam replies, *"I heard you walking in the garden, so I hid. I was afraid because I was naked"* (Genesis 3:10). God then asks them the question of the hour—a question that He is still asking: *"Who told you that you were naked?"* (Genesis 3:11). God asked them about the origin of their insecurity. He wanted to know who fractured their innocence and brought them fear and why shame now existed in two people who were created to be shameless. God wanted to know whose voice contradicted His own. *Who labeled them?*

LABELS ARE THIS FALLEN WORLD'S ATTEMPT TO CONTRADICT WHAT GOD HAS SAID ABOUT YOU.

Labels are this fallen world's attempt to contradict what God has said about you. In Genesis 3, the serpent first tells a lie about God, opening the door for more lies. Keep in mind, Adam and Eve *knew nothing but the truth.* They couldn't even conceive of lying. The devil promises them enlightenment and equality, but gives them shame and insecurity. He replaces their purity with the strong stickiness of self-doubt. Now he can label them and they can label themselves. Sin opens the door and a flood of falsehoods rush in. Labels have been sticking to mankind ever since.

"Who told you that you were naked?" is not just God's question to Adam and Eve. It's His question to *us.* This seemingly obvious question—to which God knew the answer—made it into the Bible for a reason. God knew this story would resonate with *us* when we read it. He knew we would sense our nakedness and feel shame when we rebelled against His Word. God knew we would listen to the wrong voices when it came to our self-worth.

God is still asking us to honor His voice above others' and our own. God wants to stop the lies and remove all the labels. It is crucial that we stop listening to the enemy's minimization of God's love for us. Why do we so easily accept the labels of shame? Why do we embrace insecurity rather than the security that can only be found in the love of God? Why have we replaced the voice of our Creator with another? Why do we label ourselves when He is the only one who knows who we really are? He sees our nakedness and loves us anyway. We have no reason to be afraid.

Paul wrote these encouraging words: *"God showed his great love for us by sending Christ to die for us while we were still sinners"* (Romans 5:8). Before you could remove any of your labels, He was already on His way to the cross for you. Jesus decided you were worthy of His sacrifice before you could do anything to earn it. His love for you has the power to obliterate your insecurity. Labels cannot cling to someone who knows they are perfectly loved by God. With the psalmist, we can cry out, *"The LORD is for me, so I will have no fear. What can mere people do to me?"* (Psalm 118:6). People have no real power when you embrace the reality that God has for you. Nothing anyone says about you can stick to you when you are covered in His love.

WHO HAS THE RIGHT?

I own an old-school label maker. It has a trigger that imprints one letter at a time on a plastic strip with an adhesive backing. When you're done, you have a perfect label that can be used to place a tag of ownership on just about anything.

Imagine if my label maker and I visited your house today. What if I walked right in and started labeling your stuff? Your furniture, your electronics, all your dishes—nothing would be safe. You would surely object to what I was doing! I would probably not make it past the first item before you stopped me. You'd say, "Hey, you can't do that! You can't label this, it's mine. You don't own it." Exactly. There are only two people with the right to label something: the creator and the owner. If you create something, it's your right to label it. If you purchase something or receive it as a gift, you have the right to label it as yours.

I have quoted from Ephesians 2:10 a few times, but it bears repeating: *"We are God's masterpiece. He has created us anew in Christ Jesus, so we can do the good things he planned for us long ago."* God is the Creator and we are His masterpiece. He has labeled us for *"good things"* that He planned for us long ago. Paul declared, *"God bought you with a high price. So you must honor God with your body"* (1 Corinthians 6:20). Did you catch that? God *bought* you. God *owns* you. God purchased us by sending His only Son Jesus to pay the price for our sins on a cross that *we* deserved. Our lives are not our own. This is a wonderful thing because it means we can live the rich life God wants us to have. God is both our Creator and our owner. He is the only one who has the right to label us.

When I came to Christ at age sixteen, I was covered in labels. Almost all of them were placed on me by people who did not have the right to label me. My identity was heading in a hundred different directions and none of them were taking me to where God wanted me to be. Labels are designed to highlight both the purpose and usefulness of something. If you label your toaster, you have just defined its purpose and confirmed its usefulness. When someone labels you as worthless, they are saying you have no purpose or usefulness. If you believe *that* judgment, your opportunities become limited and you start missing out on the life God has for you.

~~~~~~~~~~~~~~~

WE ALL NEED TO BECOME VERY STINGY WITH OUR *LABELING RIGHTS*. ONLY THE CREATOR HAS THE REAL PERMISSION TO DECIDE WHO YOU ARE MEANT TO BE.

~~~~~~~~~~~~~~~

We all need to become very stingy with our *labeling rights* and be selective about what voices we honor. Whoever has your permission to speak into your identity also has power over you. Only the Creator has the real permission to decide who you are meant to be. The other voices you empower should only confirm what He says about you.

It's important to note that even our own voices cannot be fully trusted. We all have the potential to be a major threat to ourselves when it comes to labeling. No one is more acquainted with the depth of your failures and the vastness of your weaknesses than you. Without an attitude of self-grace, you will get your own identity wrong every time. God sees you as redeemed, healthy, and whole. Your own view of yourself may have failed to catch up with this reality, but that does not nullify who God says you are. So read the Bible and make it personal—even placing yourself in it. When the Bible says, "*God so loved the world*" (John 3:16 NKJV), I read it as "God so loved Doug." You should do the same. You may not *feel* loved, but you *are* loved. God labels you as His beloved. You may not feel like you have a great purpose, but God says that you do. You may not think you are a *masterpiece*, but God declares that you are! His labels should replace the ones you have given yourself.

THE STRONGEST LIES TWIST THE TRUTH

Negative labels are lies. But as I mentioned earlier in the book, lies are powerful because they contain elements of truth. The strongest lies are always partially true—but they twist the truth. That's what makes labels so sticky. When someone says something bad about you, your mind partially agrees with them because there's a fraction of truth in what they said. You helplessly harmonize with the *choir* of those who refuse to believe in you. You sing their *songs* under your breath because you know you are undeserving of any form of grace.

In moments like this, you must resist their lies and remind yourself of the loving identity that your Creator has given you. Today is a good day to quit *singing their song* and start believing His *truth*. You are loved. You are His.

I love this verse from the prophet Zephaniah:

The LORD your God is living among you. He is a mighty savior. He will take delight in you with gladness. With his love, he will calm all your fears. He will rejoice over you with joyful songs.

(Zephaniah 3:17)

What is God doing right now? He is delighting over you! He is calming your fears with His love. He is singing joyful songs about you. Start singing with Him. Join His choir of grace. Celebrate yourself like He celebrates you. Allow your voice to join in with His. Sing about your potential while you forget the hopeless melodies of your dark past. Place the songs of His love for you on repeat and play them to yourself for the rest of your life. Your Creator is on your side and you have a tremendous destiny in Him. His labels are the only ones that matter.

WHAT THE KING SAYS

I don't talk a lot about dreams or visions. I have an aversion to weirdness and some have abused the privilege of telling us their strange dreams. Not every dream has meaning and not every undisciplined thought is a vision. Sometimes, you just should not eat pizza before you go to bed! Sometimes, your unruly thoughts should be ignored. In several places, however, the Bible does show us that God can and will speak to us in this way. The best advice I can give is that a vision or dream from God should be in alignment with Scripture and it must be confirmed by the Holy Spirit. It must lift up and not tear down. It is also important to note that this is not the normative way God speaks to us. God communicating to a person through a dream or vision is a rare thing. With those balancing truths in place, let me tell you a true story.

About fifteen years ago, my summer was packed with camps and short-term mission trips. About three weeks into my schedule, after speaking to a group of students and leaders, I called them all forward to pray. They responded passionately and God was moving in our midst, healing hearts and minds. I was simply praying from the stage, without using the microphone because no direction was needed. God was doing a great work that night. Then it happened—a vision filled my mind. It was like I was suddenly wearing a virtual reality headset and a video was playing that only I could see. In the vision, I saw a poor young man entering what appeared to be a royal throne room in a castle. He was obviously a pauper, but he was being ushered into this large space that was adorned in gold and glorious artwork. He was awkward and scared, but he was also in awe of what he was seeing.

A large throne was the only piece of furniture in the room. Sitting there with complete confidence was a majestic king. At first, his image was blurry...but then I could see his face. He exuded strength. He had love in his demeanor and amusement in his eyes. The young man was so taken by the majesty of the room that he had not noticed the king. After a few moments, the king began to laugh at the fact that he had not been recognized. He then called out to the young man and told him to come forward. The man walked cautiously toward the throne and stood there in utter amazement. The king was only a few feet away from him. How did he deserve such an honor? He was overwhelmed.

The king said, "What might I do for you today?" The young man began to urgently search his mind for the words to respond. He mentally struggled for several minutes. Then he reluctantly replied, "Sir, your majesty, I am so embarrassed. I have forgotten why I am here." The young man was so taken with the mere fact that he was in the king's presence in this magnificent room that his mind had gone blank. The king broke out in passionate laughter. All the visitors to his throne were always meticulously prepared and had plenty of requests. Now, here was a young man so enthralled that he could barely function. This moved the king's heart.

The king arose from his throne and graciously approached the young man. He told him to kneel before him. He bent over and began to quietly whisper in his ear. I could not hear what the king was saying, but I somehow knew that his words were filled with life. The young man cried and nodded his head in agreement. Somehow I knew that the young man was being told who he was. The king was gently declaring to this young man who he would become. The king spoke directly to his unformed identity. After a few moments, the king lifted the young man to his feet, hugged him, and sent him on his way. Vision over.

This is the vision that God gave me. Over the next few months, at different times and occasions, I experienced the exact same detailed vision at least a dozen times. Each time, it was involuntary and each time, it impacted me to my core. By that fall of that same year, the vision stopped coming to me. I have prayed about the vision and asked the Holy Spirit to show me what it meant. I have received a lot of direction from Him, some of which is too personal to write about.

JESUS IS THE KING WHO TELLS US WHO WE ARE AND WHAT WE WILL BE.

Here is what I believe to be the spiritual significance of that vision: we have a King and His name is Jesus. We are the paupers and He is the King. His voice carries royal weight and authority. He is the one who tells us who we are and what we will be. He alone forms our identities. He is the King of Kings. When we enter His presence, we are enthralled with Him and He speaks to us. His words are life itself.

I have thought a lot about what must have happened next for the young man in my vision. The vision was always the same—he would receive a Word from the King and he would leave. I was never shown what happened next. But I imagine that the young man had lots of obstructive voices in his life. If he is anything like us, he probably was wearing a lot of labels when he walked into that throne room. I have a feeling that his labels fell off in the presence of the King. I bet he walked away from that throne room a free man. I think he lived differently after that encounter. I think his life was elevated and he became who the King said he was.

Imagine with me for a moment. What if the young man went home and told his family what happened? We can surmise that his story would be hard to believe. How does a pauper end up in the presence of a King? His family would probably tell him to stop dreaming and get back in his place with everyone else. They would remind him that he was not that special. But the young man would *mentally relive* his encounter with royalty. He had been with King and the King had spoken to him.

What if he got the same reaction from his teachers, his coworkers, and his friends? He would have to decide which voices to believe. People want to keep us in the box they have known us to be in. People love to categorize. So the labelers of this young man's life would probably work overtime to *reglue* his old identity on him. He would now have to decide who to believe: the King or everyone else?

In my mind, I have him standing strong for the rest of his days. He does not have to lash out at those who would try to hold him back. Their insecurities are not his problem to solve. No, he can now live in quiet confidence because he has been in the King's presence. Over time, he develops an "I was with the King" reflex. It goes like this: as someone tries to label him, all he does is compare it to what the King said. If it does not line up, he can quickly dismiss it as the lie that it is. He has been transformed and a different life is possible. The King has spoken. No label could ever compare with the power of His words.

LISTEN TO THE KING, NOT THE LABELERS

What if we all decided to live like this—if, from this day forward, we decided to hand our *label makers* to the King? When someone says something that contradicts what the King has said about us, we reject it quietly and quickly. Our identities are now set by what the King has said about us. A different life would be possible. We could live the life He always intended for us to have. This would greatly please the King.

Paul encouraged his friends:

Continue to work out your salvation with fear and trembling, for it is God who works in you to will and to act in order to fulfill his good purpose. Do everything without grumbling or arguing, so that you may become blameless and pure, "children of God without fault in a warped and crooked generation." Then you will shine among them like stars in the sky as you hold firmly to the word of life.

(Philippians 2:12–16 NIV)

There is a lot of truth there, but let me break it down. It's important to *rehearse* the fact that you are extravagantly loved by God. You *"work out your salvation"* by daily reminding yourself that you and your life are His. Stop waiting for a better opportunity! Now is the time *"to will and to act"* in accordance with the *"good purpose"* God has for us. We must live out what the King has said. We need to align our voices with His, instead of *"grumbling or arguing."* If we do this, we will shine *"like the stars in the sky"* in this *"warped"* generation we live in. This generation is warped because it has been labeled. Even the labelers have been labeled. The only way to help them is to live differently among them. This is what the King would want us to do.

~~~~~~~

THIS GENERATION IS WARPED BECAUSE IT HAS BEEN LABELED. EVEN THE LABELERS HAVE BEEN LABELED. THE ONLY WAY TO HELP THEM IS TO LIVE DIFFERENTLY AMONG THEM.

~~~~~~~

I want you to embrace the last phrase: *"as you hold firmly to the word of life."* Another translation says, *"Carry the light-giving Message into the night"* (MSG). Incorporate this into your thinking. *"Hold firmly to the word of life"*—the King's Word—and carry it into this darkness that surrounds us.

Think of yourself as a climber and what God has said about you is the rope that you're hanging on to for dear life. God wants you to apply His loving word to yourself. He has already spoken! The Bible is filled with what the King has said about you. Let the Holy Spirit apply God's unchanging Word to your wounded identity. The King knows who you are meant to be. *His* labels bring life.

GENERATIONAL LABELS

I recently read about two homeless brothers who, along with their sister, inherited four billion British pounds. They were so poor that they lived in a cave outside Budapest, Hungary, and sold the scrap they found on the streets to survive. They had been estranged from their wealthy mother, but when she died, they received her fortune. Everything changed for them because they inherited what was already theirs. Then I read another story about a homeless man in Bolivia who inherited $6 million from his ex-wife. But when the police approached him to tell him the good news, he fled. He thought he was going to be arrested. Tragically, they never found him. One inheritance was received and one was lost. These contrasting stories sound a lot like our own lives.[4]

Labels have an isolating effect. When we are labeled, we can find ourselves living inside the *caves* of what others have said about us. We tragically live below the *wealth* that belongs to us. We *run away* because we can't believe there's good news for us.

Removing our labels can be a scary thing because anything that sticks on you can become a comfort. Even a false identity puts an end to the exhaustion of searching for who you are. So you decorate the cave and crawl inside. You pick a patch of dirt and sleep on it. You're not home, but what other choice do you have? This is the dilemma that false labels put us in. They make us live a life we were not meant to live. But the misery can end. We can stop running and start receiving.

The Bible tells us, *"Because we are united with Christ, we have received an inheritance from God, for he chose us in advance, and he makes everything work out according to his plan"* (Ephesians 1:11). We have an *"inheritance from God."* We are wealthy in Christ. We have been *chosen* by God and He has promised us that He will make *"everything work out according to his plan."* The word *inheritance* is a legal term. It is typically used to tell someone that they are receiving something because they are part of a family. Just a few verses earlier Paul wrote, *"God decided in advance to adopt us into his own family by bringing us to himself through Jesus Christ. This is what he wanted to do, and it gave him great pleasure"* (Ephesians 1:5). It is God's great pleasure to adopt us into His family. We have an inheritance because we have been adopted by Him.

---

4. "10 Unbelievable Inheritance Stories," Oddee blog, www.oddee.com/item_96948.aspx; accessed January 23, 2019.

All of this inheritance talk is great news...but there is another side to this issue. You can inherit good things, but you also can inherit bad things. In several places in the Old Testament, we read that *iniquity* can extend to three or four generations. (See, for example, Exodus 34:7; Numbers 14:18; Deuteronomy 5:9.) *The International Standard Bible Encyclopedia* tells us that the word *iniquity* is used hundreds of times in the Old Testament and means "crooked or perverse."[5] It's a *lean* or a *bent* in the direction of sin. Iniquity perverts what God intended to be perfect and it damages us in ways that extend beyond our personal sin. Iniquity itself is a thief because it's an inclination to sin. Iniquity is one of the ways we rob ourselves of the life God intended us to have.

THE INSANE CYCLE OF INIQUITY CONTINUES FROM ONE GENERATION TO THE NEXT UNTIL SOMEONE BREAKS IT THROUGH THE POWER OF JESUS CHRIST.

But iniquity has a deeper origin than its effects on one individual. It's a generational plague transferred through a family line, a tendency toward destructive behavior, insecurity, or a bent toward an evil that can destroy *you*. Maybe your father was negatively labeled by *his* father's sin and he in turn was negatively labeled by your great-grandfather's perverse ways. Now, four generations later, the label has been passed down to you. Iniquity brings inherited coping mechanisms leading you away from the life you were ordained to live. This insane cycle continues from one generation to the next until someone breaks it through the power of Jesus Christ. Iniquity loses its adhesiveness when it encounters His love.

I'm pretty sure you already know what iniquity there is in your family. The pattern is obvious if you pay attention. Addiction, sexual sin, relational

---

5. www.biblestudytools.com/dictionary/iniquity.

dysfunction, low self-worth, and other manifestations of moral corruption raise their ugly heads from generation to generation. What we call "societal issues" are really generational problems. If it seems like things are getting worse, it's because they are. The longer sins hang around, the stronger they become. If a label sticks to something long enough, it can fuse itself in a way that makes it almost impossible to remove. But the destruction can end with *your* generation. No label is resilient enough to keep your Savior from removing it! A label's longevity does not make it exempt from the truth of your freedom in Christ. The generational insanity *can* and *will* stop with you!

God tells us He will *"lavish unfailing love for a thousand generations on those who love me and obey my commands"* (Exodus 20:6). David wrote, *"The love of the LORD remains forever with those who fear him. His salvation extends to the children's children of those who are faithful to his covenant, of those who obey his commandments!"* (Psalm 103:17–18). Your descendants are depending on *you* to remove the lasting negative labels of your family's legacy. Your destiny in Jesus is not just about you. Your present and future family is affected by your freedom. Your new legacy depends on the removal of old labels.

I mentioned John, *the disciple who Jesus loved*, in a previous chapter. How that *title*—a wonderful label—came about is a curious truth, but it has a powerful meaning. John was one of four disciples who were inspired by the Holy Spirit to write an eyewitness account of the ministry of Jesus. Strangely enough, in his book, John actually labels himself. He uses a defining statement to tell us where he draws his identity from. Writing about a dinner with Jesus, John said, *"One of them, the disciple whom Jesus loved, was reclining next to him"* (John 13:23 NIV). John is talking about himself! But instead of giving us his name, he calls himself *"the disciple whom Jesus loved."* Now that's a great label!

YOU ARE HIS FAVORITE!

One might think John is trying to lift himself above the other disciples, but that's not what is happening here. However, I do believe John is saying he just might be Jesus's favorite! It sounds wrong...until you contemplate the love of Jesus. His love is so boundless that He can love all of us fully and completely at the same time. We can *all* be His favorites—I can be His favorite and so can you! I am the *disciple who Jesus loves*—and so are you.

John is not comparing himself to anyone; he is just declaring a beautiful fact. Jesus loved John. That was John's label and it should be yours too. That's a great label for us to pass down to future generations. Jesus loves us. We are His favorites.

DISCOVERY QUESTIONS

What are some false labels sticking on you?

_____

_____

_____

_____

How has your insecurity given others permission to label you? What can you do about it?

_____

_____

_____

_____

What has the King said about you and your future?

_____

_____

_____

_____

How can we break the generational curse of iniquity or patterns of sin?

_____

_____

_____

_____

EIGHT

RUN YOUR RACE

Strip down, start running—and never quit!
—Hebrews 12:1 (MSG)

The only time I ever quit was during gym class. It was a beautiful fall morning at the beginning of my sophomore year at a public high school. That day, our gym coach had decided to evaluate the fitness level of our class. He took all of us out to the quarter-mile, cinder-covered track that encircled the football field. After splitting up the guys and the girls, he told us we were to run a mile—four full laps around the track—as fast as we could. But since this was a fitness test, if we were too tired to go on, we could simply *quit*. He should have never mentioned that word because the idea of quitting spread like a disease among the class. Everyone was *too cool* to try their hardest, but quitting would project the proper level of carelessness. Collectively, the class turned the option to quit into an invitation to give up.

The girls ran first. To no one's surprise, after only one lap, all the girls decided they were too tired to go on. Now it was our turn. As the guys were preparing, my classmate Todd began to challenge me. Todd and I had been in several gym classes together and had developed a bit of a rivalry.

Whatever we were doing, we would compete against each other. Todd was the better athlete, so he would always win. But that summer, I had been running and playing multiple sports, so I was in good shape. As the guys approached the line, Todd asked me if I was going to quit. I said, "No way" and so our epic race was on. At first, we simply paced with the other guys, but after a couple of laps, they all quit. Todd and I kept running and engaging in a bit of trash talk. This was now a two-man contest.

Around the three-quarter mile mark, I noticed Todd was beginning to struggle. Running reveals what is going on inside of you. No matter how cool you are, you cannot stay composed when you're losing your stamina. I thought to myself, *I'm not even tired yet! I'm going to win this race and finally beat Todd!* My plan was to let him keep up with me until there was only a hundred yards left to go, when I would turn on the jets and blow him off the track in dramatic fashion. This was my day! But as we approached the final stretch of the final lap, I could hear cheering in the distance. Todd and I were suddenly aware that the rest of the class was watching our seemingly neck and neck, two-man race. Everyone was cheering…but they were not cheering for me.

SOMETHING BROKE INSIDE ME

I could clearly hear the class screaming Todd's name over and over again. He was way more popular than I was and the closer we got to the end of our race, the louder and more excited the cheers became. I think I even heard the teacher call out Todd's name. I thought, *That's just not right! How did I get myself into this?* It was all happening so fast, but it affected me deeply. This season of my life was a couple of months before I gave my heart to Christ. My self-worth was incredibly low and I felt hopeless about my future. So a whole class of my peers cheering for my opponent was more than I could take. Something inside of me broke. I lost the willpower to go on. I'm embarrassed to say it, but about fifty yards from the finish line, I gave up. I quit. I thought, *If you want Todd to win, then fine.* I waited until about twenty yards out and I intentionally backed off a step. Todd passed by me and won our race.

That's the only time in my entire life I can ever remember quitting on anything. Of course, I moved on from there and a couple of months later, my best friend invited me to church. I accepted his invitation, heard about the matchless love of Jesus for the first time, and became utterly and completely transformed. A few years later, I headed off to college and the meaningless race from a high school gym class was the furthest thing from my mind. But God has a way of using the traumatic events of our past to grow us. Three years after my race with Todd, a few months into my freshman year, I returned home for a visit. My old church youth group was attending our local high school football game and I decided to join them.

We were among the last people to leave that night. I was trailing behind, walking on the very track where I had quit my race with Todd. Something triggered my memories of that day. Perhaps it was the sound of cinders beneath my feet, or the smell of grass from the field. Whatever it was, God transported me back in time. The flashback was like a private documentary playing before my eyes and I relived every moment of the race. I could hear my classmates cheering for Todd and I recalled how it made me feel. I saw myself quitting and losing on purpose. Then, I sensed the Holy Spirit speaking. In my heart and mind, I clearly heard, "I do not ever want you to do that again." I knew right away that God was not just talking about track races. I felt compelled to reply. Without caring who heard me, I yelled out: "I will never do that again!" It's a commitment to God that I have kept. I have *not* quit. I will *never* quit.

YOU CAN GROW IN BOTH VICTORY
AND IN DEFEAT, BUT QUITTING IS ALWAYS
INFERTILE GROUND, SABOTAGING ANY
POSSIBILITY OF GROWTH.

There is a quitting crisis in our culture today. As a society, we have become comfortable with resignation. We have made peace with giving up. We see this unhealthy trend in every arena of life. Our revised motto goes like this,

"When the going gets tough, the tough stop trying." I am not talking about failing, which is not the same at all. You can try your hardest and still fail—but you don't give up. Failure builds character. Quitting destroys the soul. When you choose to quit, you take over the outcome and kill your chance of winning, losing, or growing. You can grow in both victory and in defeat, but quitting is always infertile ground, sabotaging any possibility of growth.

I quit my race with Todd because I had labeled myself as *unworthy of winning*. I owned the label maker and I used it against myself. Three years after that race, I wished I could have a do-over. I really believed the cheers against me then would make me run even faster. I wished I could break the hearts of the entire class by blowing Todd off the track.

But that history has already been written. Now, the scar that quitting has left on me is my motivation to never quit again. I have torn off the label of unworthiness and replaced it with the perfect love of my Savior. My pursuit for Him is now relentless. He never quit on me and I will never quit on Him.

THEY ARE CHEERING FOR YOU

The Olympics are taking place as I write this chapter. People from all over the world are *running their races* and being cheered on by their countries. No matter what the sport, they are competing for the prize. A lot has changed since the Olympics began in 776 B.C. in Olympia, Greece. The athletes then were all male citizens of the city-states from every corner of the Greek world, coming from as far away as Iberia (Spain) in the west and the Black Seas (Turkey) in the east.[6] The Olympics are a Greek-born tradition.

The New Testament Bible was originally written in koine Greek, the common language of the eastern Mediterranean. Other than the Gospels, most of the New Testament took place in and around Greece. While reading the New Testament, you will find *Olympic terminology* being used, especially by the apostle Paul:

6. "The Real Story of the Ancient Olympic Games," University of Pennsylvania Museum of Archaeology and Anthropology, www.penn.museum/sites/olympics/olympicorigins.shtml, accessed January 26, 2019.

You've all been to the stadium and seen the athletes race. Everyone runs; one wins. Run to win. All good athletes train hard. They do it for a gold medal that tarnishes and fades. You're after one that's gold eternally.   (1 Corinthians 9:24–25 MSG)

I have fought the good fight, I have finished the race, and I have remained faithful.   (2 Timothy 4:7)

Paul lived in a culture of competition and it seems he was a fan of the Olympics.

God wants *us* to run our races. The writer of Hebrews wrote a whole chapter that biblical scholars affectionately call the *Hall of Fame of Faith*. It reminds us of heroes of faith like Noah, Abraham, Isaac, Jacob, Moses, David, and more. The writer concludes his thoughts on these amazing people, telling us they *"were all commended for their faith"* (Hebrews 11:39 NIV). Just when you wonder where the author is going, he connects us with the bold faith of our ancient heroes. They ran a great race, but their race has ended. They are now in the heavenly stadium cheering us on. *"Therefore, since we are surrounded by such a great cloud of witnesses, let us throw off everything that hinders and the sin that so easily entangles. And let us run with perseverance the race marked out for us"* (Hebrews 12:1 NIV). Another translation says, *"We have such a huge crowd of men of faith watching us from the grandstands"* (TLB). Those who have gone before us are watching us run our race with great anticipation.

I picture us on the race track at Olympia Stadium and as we run our race, the past champions are giving out *high fives* and maybe even *doing the wave*. They are cheering *for us*. Past generations of faith are engaged in our struggle. Hebrews 12:1 tells us that we are connected to the faith-filled men and women of the past. We are not running an independent race; instead, we're in a relay event. We have taken the baton from those who ran before us and we are running the same race in our generation. Your *stadium* is full today. Maybe no one is cheering for you in this life, but you have a huge, heavenly audience. The heroes of the Bible and everyone who's gone before you surround you as you run your race. They are depending on you. Do not quit!

~~~

MAYBE NO ONE IS CHEERING FOR YOU IN THIS LIFE, BUT YOU HAVE A HUGE, HEAVENLY AUDIENCE. THE HEROES OF THE BIBLE ARE DEPENDING ON YOU. DO NOT QUIT!

~~~

Maybe no one from your family *ran their race* of faith. Maybe you are the first one to do so. You may not feel any *wind of encouragement* at your back from those who are supposed to be there for you. Perhaps everyone you know has quit on you. Know this: you have spiritual lineage that you can claim as your own. John explained how this is possible when he wrote, *"To all who did receive him, to those who believed in his name, he gave the right to become children of God—children born not of natural descent, nor of human decision or a husband's will, but born of God"* (John 1:12–13 NIV).

You have been born into the family of God through Christ. This fact is not subject to biological realities. It's a spiritual reality that is higher than your earthly lineage. You are a child of God. Therefore, you are related to every person of faith who has gone before you. Your long-lost heavenly relatives are cheering for you. *I* am cheering for you. We are in this race together. You do not run alone.

RUN FREE OF BURDENS

The letter to the Hebrews says, *"Let us throw off everything that hinders and the sin that so easily entangles. And let us run with perseverance the race marked out for us"* (Hebrews 12:1 NIV). If you are going to run well, you have to shed whatever slows your pace. You have to lay down the heavy burdens of this life. Olympic athletes wear expensive uniforms that are strategically designed to reduce resistance—because resistance kills speed and keeps people from running their race.

In my race against Todd, my baggy 1983 running shorts were not the *resistance* that was holding me back. I was handicapped by the false identities I was carrying in my own heart and mind. Those heavy self-judgments affected the way I ran. My sin had also entangled me and was slowing me down. David wrote this about the weight of sin:

> *There is no soundness in my bones because of my sin. My guilt has overwhelmed me like a burden too heavy to bear.*
>
> (Psalm 38:3–4 NIV)

This is a picture of a man struggling beneath a heavy weight. David's sin was costing him his race. Sin will do the same to us if we let it. The good news is, Christ took our sins to the cross so we can freely run our race. He carried the heavy encumbrances of our lives, so we don't have to. Jesus says, *"Come to me, all you who are weary and burdened, and I will give you rest"* (Matthew 11:28 NIV). Jesus offers us the rest our souls long for. We can run free because He has replaced the weights we were carrying with His grace and His rest.

I'm comforted by the last line of Hebrews 12:1: *"And let us run with perseverance the race marked out for us."* To persevere, we must have a clear vision of where we are going. Those who have gone before you have created a trail that you can follow. This *race* has been *marked out* for you. God has dreamed up your journey and it's now your time to run. If you quit early, you will never discover His *divine intentions* for your life that await during the *next lap*. Get up and keep running. *"Though the righteous fall seven times, they rise again"* (Proverbs 24:16 NIV). Whatever knocked you down lacks the power to keep you down. Today is your day to rise and get back in your race.

DESIGNED FOR VICTORY

I go deer hunting every fall. I enjoy hunting, but what I like the most is just being in the woods. A few years ago, I was spending long days in a tree stand waiting for a trophy buck to walk by. I was communicating with God while I waited and He began to speak to me in a soft, gentle inner voice that resounded in my very soul. I sensed the Lord saying, "Count the V's." *What?* I didn't know what He meant. But I heard the phrase in my spirit several times. *Count the V's.* Not knowing what else to do, I started looking around, pondering these words. Then it struck me. There are no perfectly horizontal lines in nature. That's why it's easy to get lost in a forest and why a man-made structure like a tree stand is easy to spot.

I counted hundreds of V-shaped branches just in the tree I was sitting in. As I expanded my view, I thought, *There must be hundreds of thousands of V's in this little patch of woods alone. There must be billions of V's in the vast forest surrounding me.* At that moment, God spoke to my spirit again. He said, "Your natural state is victory. I designed you to live in victory." Right away, I understood what God was saying. God made me to be victorious. This realization filled me with joy. That was a good day in the woods.

God's message about *the V's* has stayed with me. Every time I start to feel defeated, I remember that God designed me to be victorious in Him. John writes about our victory:

Every child of God defeats this evil world, and we achieve this victory through our faith. And who can win this battle against the world? Only those who believe that Jesus is the Son of God. (1 John 5:4–5)

When we place our faith in Jesus, we are no longer defeated by the broken systems of this world. Because Christ overcame the world and even death itself, you and I can live a victorious life. You can *run the race* and you can win. Your *supernatural* state is victory!

Everyone wants to win. We may learn something when we lose, but it's never fun. Winning teaches you and gives you pleasure at the same time. Winning is just better than losing. I think the apostle Paul agrees with me because he writes, *"Don't you realize that in a race everyone runs, but only one person gets the prize? So run to win!"* (1 Corinthians 9:24). Paul was no advocate of holding back—he wanted us to run like winners. I think the first step to victory is believing that you are *supposed to win*. God *wants* you to win. You will never run in victory if you believe you are only worthy of defeat. To develop a winning attitude, you must reject all of the *losing mindsets* you have developed. You will never run in victory if you believe you are only worthy of defeat.

BECAUSE CHRIST OVERCAME THE WORLD
AND EVEN DEATH ITSELF,
YOU AND I CAN LIVE A VICTORIOUS LIFE.
YOU CAN *RUN THE RACE* AND YOU CAN WIN.
YOUR *SUPERNATURAL* STATE IS VICTORY!

Every good coach in every sport believes what I just wrote. If you believe you're going to lose, that's exactly what will happen. If you've ever played on any team, or competed in any way, you probably heard a motivational speech or two. A big part of the coach's job is helping you believe you can win. Sports psychologists call this *visualization*. It means that your performance is a product of what's happening in your head. Your coach might point at his head and say, "What happens out there is a result of what's happening in here." You must believe it to receive it. We should be like a world-class runner who mentally wins a race before he ever steps on the track. He visualizes himself running his best race and talks himself past his pain before he even begins. While others are backing off, he has prepared his mind and body to press harder. He prepares himself to win.

Have you prepared yourself to win your race...or lose it? What attitude have you embraced as you enter your personal arena? Your thoughts will determine your outcome. Winning happens in the mind before the starter pistol is ever fired.

After Paul tells us to *"run to win,"* he tells us that those who run the race receive a reward.

*All athletes are disciplined in their training. They do it to win a prize
that will fade away, but we do it for an eternal prize. So I run with
purpose in every step.*   (1 Corinthians 9:25–26)

Paul is telling us that if athletes spend excessive amounts of time disci-
plining and conditioning themselves to win *earthly* prizes, how much more
should we prepare ourselves for the race that has a *heavenly* reward? Most
people *run* like they have no purpose—because they don't even know God
has one for them. *But you do.* God wants you to run in a way that honors
His *divine intentions* for you. You must run to win.

All of this talk of winning can make you think you are in a competition—but your victory is not about finishing ahead of others. You're not
meant to push others down as you race past them. No, the prize waiting for
you at the end of your well-run race is the rich fulfillment of living the life
you were meant to have. Shedding the weight of your insecurities means
you get to stop competing and start loving. You get your second wind by
giving life to others. This is when running becomes fun! Your freedom will
blaze a trail for others to follow. Your victory has the power to pull them
out of their defeat.

QUIT ON QUITTING

At the beginning of this chapter, I told you about an unexpected *fitness
test* race in my high school gym class. It's ironic, but I had a very similar
experience in grade school. This is one of my earliest childhood memories.
Just like my future high school coach, our gym teacher wanted to see what
kind of shape his young athletes were in. He had us line up against the gym
wall and challenged us to run circles around the basketball court until we
were too tired to continue. The last one to quit would be the winner. After
the teacher's short inspirational speech, we began to run.

This was a straight-forward exercise, a simple test of body, mind, and
spirit. I was quite young at the time, but as I leaned against the wall and
listened, I remember processing the gym teacher's words. They made sense
and motivated me: "Don't quit and you win." I had never won anything,
but I could do this. I was not the best athlete, but this test did not require

talent or skill. In my mind, it was just a matter of will. I thought to myself, *I won't quit. I can win this.*

We started running laps around that small gym. It didn't matter if we ran fast or slow. Everyone tried to do their best at first, then kids started to drop out. When the first one did, it seemed like a quitting spirit permeated the air. Each one who quit gave someone else permission to do the same. Finally, there were only five or six left. Then there were three…then two… and then just me. That's right: I won that race, although it was not really a race. It was just a test of will. Something inside me clicked that day. I knew I possessed a stubborn perseverance that made me special. I knew other people could be more gifted—but I was *not* a quitter.

Of course, years later, on the high school track, I went against my own spirit. It was the only time I ever quit, but for some people, once is all it takes to be a lifelong quitter. If I had not met Christ a couple of months later, I believe that my one moment of quitting would have triggered an avalanche of giving up for the rest of my life. When Jesus redeemed me, He halted what could have been a plague. He brought me back to who I was created to be.

Quitting is not something you are born with, it's something you develop. A baby won't stop crying until he is comforted or fed. A toddler will beg you for what he wants until you give it to him or discipline him. And kids will run around a gym until they drop, just because a teacher said it was the right thing to do. Quitting did not come naturally to me, it was something I learned. But our tendency to relinquish can be unlearned and replaced with the persistence we were born to have.

The day I returned to my high school race track was the day I quit on quitting. This is something every one of us must do. But first, we may need to reverse-engineer the problem by taking a journey into our past to diagnose what went wrong. The unrelenting determination that came so easily to me in grade school is not hard to explain. I could run far and long because I was running without a heavy load. I was too young to carry many labels— most of those would come later. I was not weighted down by worry, hurt, or responsibility. I had never experienced failure. I approached running with naivety and my innocence energized me. Things were simple: *Run, do not quit, and you will win.* That childhood reality is now my adult philosophy. I am already victorious in Christ, so if I do not quit, I will win! We need to return to that childhood mind-set and learn how to run free again.

Runners must focus and live fully in the moment in order to win the race. In grade school, I had no problem with that. I was not thinking about the past or the future. But as an adult, living in the moment is difficult. I overthink when I should be concentrating on the race. I look back when I should be focusing forward. Jesus warned, *"Anyone who puts a hand to the plow and then looks back is not fit for the Kingdom of God"* (Luke 9:62). The imagery here is powerful. In biblical times, plowing was done manually with a plow and oxen. If you did not look straight ahead, you ended up with uneven rows, robbing you of your best possible harvest. When we fail to focus, we diminish the rewards that we were meant to have. We run slower and we win less often.

WHEN WE FAIL TO FOCUS, WE DIMINISH THE REWARDS THAT WE WERE MEANT TO HAVE. WE RUN SLOWER AND WE WIN LESS OFTEN.

If you want to *quit on quitting*, then change your focus.

We do this by keeping our eyes on Jesus, the champion who initiates and perfects our faith. Because of the joy awaiting him, he endured the cross, disregarding its shame. Now he is seated in the place of honor beside God's throne. Think of all the hostility he endured from sinful people; then you won't become weary and give up. (Hebrews 12:2–3)

When we focus on the wrong things, we tire easily and are prone to quitting. But when we focus on Jesus and consider all that He endured for us, we are rejuvenated with His strength. *"He endured the cross, disregarding its shame."* That fact should be our focus. His endurance is our motivation. When we embrace this, even our difficult races will be put in their proper place. A humble perspective makes you run farther and faster. When you embrace the fact that *He did not quit on you*, it empowers you to never quit on Him.

THE TRYING TRAP

I love golf…and I hate it. I think most golfers have this kind of tension with the sport. I love golf because there is nothing like the feeling of hitting a good shot. The club does its job and the swing feels effortless, like poetry in motion. You swing the club and the ball goes further than you ever thought it could. I love those kinds of shots. On the other hand, I hate those kinds of shots because it's so hard to consistently make them. Occasional players like me must live off their highlight reels. A rare good shot erases the memory of the many bad ones. Your best moments keep you coming back for more abuse. Golf can make you question your sanity.

I golf with a friend who is much better at the game than me. He is my golf hero and mentor. He often tells me I'm "swinging too hard." He says I need to "let the club do the work." I love and hate that statement. It's wonderful to think that less energy could produce better results, but it's frustrating to realize that trying harder will hurt my game instead of helping it. I once heard a golf instructor say, "There is only two inches in the entire arc of a golf swing that will produce a proper golf shot." Golfers know what he's talking about. We have all struck beautiful shots where you don't even feel the ball. You find the place of power at the bottom of the arc where the club's design is maximized. Most golfers only find that place occasionally… and usually by accident. But effortless shots like that will make you head to the course again and again.

As you may have suspected, I am not just talking about golf, I'm talking about life. What if you could live your life inside the *two inches* of a perfect shot? If you stopped over-swinging and just *let the club do the work?* If you started playing smarter instead of harder? If less effort could produce much better results? If you and I lived like that, I think we would *hit better shots* and live better lives. I think we would enjoy *the game* more often and have energy to spare.

Now, enough about golf—let's get back to running. I think most of us are running our race at the wrong pace. We're running like the race of our lives will never be won unless we're dashing madly forward as fast as we can. The truth is, more effort will not make us run better. What we need is more grace, not a faster race. Grace in your pace will always win the race.

MORE EFFORT WILL NOT MAKE US RUN BETTER. WHAT WE NEED IS MORE GRACE, NOT A FASTER RACE. GRACE IN YOUR PACE WILL ALWAYS WIN THE RACE.

The Bible often speaks about the *pace of grace*, telling us:

God saved you by his grace when you believed. And you can't take credit for this; it is a gift from God. Salvation is not a reward for the good things we have done, so none of us can boast about it.

(Ephesians 2:8–9)

I also love this translation of these verses:

Saving is all his idea, and all his work. All we do is trust him enough to let him do it. It's God's gift from start to finish! We don't play the major role. If we did, we'd probably go around bragging that we'd done the whole thing! No, we neither make nor save ourselves. God does both the making and saving.

(MSG)

It is by God's amazing grace that we are saved. Every new believer in Jesus instinctively knows they did not save themselves. We all begin our race in the *two inches of a perfect swing* that only Jesus can provide. His grace is our starting point and it's what sustains us as we run for Him. A lot of races are lost because they violated this principle. If you abandon grace, you will lose your race.

If we are not careful, what begins with God's grace can quickly turn toward self-effort. The *race of grace* can become *I have to keep the pace*. We can deceive ourselves into a false assumption, a belief that we are required to maintain what God started. The book of Galatians displays an example of what I am talking about. The Galatian church was birthed by grace, but as it grew, they tragically combined aspects of Old Testament law with New Testament grace. They were saved by Jesus, but then they took upon themselves a bogus responsibility of maintaining their salvation. Addressing this issue, Paul wrote, *"It is for freedom that Christ has set us free. Stand firm, then, and do not let yourselves be burdened again by a yoke of slavery"* (Galatians 5:1 NIV). This verse tells us that the freedom produced by grace is something you *stand* in, not something you strive for. Anything less is *slavery*. The Galatian church traded freedom for the bondage of religion. They were no longer running a *race of grace*.

The apostle told them, *"You were running a good race. Who cut in on you to keep you from obeying the truth?"* (Galatians 5:7 NIV). The Galatian church had been *running a good race* in the power and at the pace that Jesus provided through the Holy Spirit. Then a religious lie deceived them, causing them to trade the freedom of grace for the friction of law. The weight of their race was now fully on them. They must have forgotten the impossible burdens of the law. Now, rather than *running by faith* in the One who saved them, they thought their own excessive efforts would make them run better. Nothing could be more untrue. Only the grace of God can keep you on pace in your race.

Once you run by the power of God's grace, you will never want to run any other way. When you experience grace, nothing less will satisfy. *Grace-filled running* shifts your faith from a responsibility to a relationship. Instead of *working your way through your weaknesses*, grace allows you to bring them to your Savior. He turns your inadequacies into advantages and you end up running faster. Your running is fueled by the fact that you are perfectly loved. Grace gives you courage, like an invigorating wind at your back. His grace is your secret to victory. You become healthy and whole because you are not always worn out from personal effort. You are empowered instead of exhausted. Jesus wants to run your race with you. He wants His presence to fill up every step of your journey. No one can teach you to run like He can.

DISCOVERY QUESTIONS

What happens to your soul when you quit?

_____

_____

_____

_____

_____

How can you walk daily in the natural state of victory Jesus has given you?

_____

_____

_____

_____

_____

What can you do to break a pattern of quitting?

_____

_____

_____

_____

_____

How can you stop "trying too hard" and live within the grace Jesus has provided?

_____

_____

_____

_____

_____

NINE

GOD THOUGHTS

*No mind has imagined what God has
prepared for those who love him.*
—1 Corinthians 2:9

As babies, each of our three kids were addicted to their pacifiers. When I say addicted, I mean a *need to go into rehab* kind of obsession. Our special nickname for pacifiers was *pappies*. As parents, our motives were pure enough—we just wanted our little ones to have a way to soothe themselves, especially when they were teething. But over time, each of our children developed an overdependence on this kid-comforting and parent sanity-saving invention. At about eighteen months, we stopped the madness with our first two children by making them go *cold turkey* and give up their pappies. There were a couple of rough nights, but soon, the crying would end and peace would return to our lives. Our rehabilitation method worked great until our last child came along. She was especially obsessed with her pappies. She loved them on a level that made our first two kids look like amateurs. It was really our fault. We were the *dealers* who caused our little one to get hooked on this seemingly harmless habit. My wife and I knew that our third child was our final baby, so we lingered too long in each stage of her development. We let her addiction to pappies grow into a monster.

Things came to a head when she was two and a half years old. Our baby was now a toddler and her pappies were a part of her blossoming personality. She carried around not one pappie but four, each one a different color. She gave each one a name, played with them, and used them to fall asleep. She would softly rub her adorable little nose with one of her pappies until she dozed off.

That summer, I took my family to a camp that I was speaking at in Wisconsin. We stayed in a beautiful cabin beside a lake. Then tragedy struck. Our toddler lost one of her favorite pacifiers. She cried while the rest of us searched. We all looked for over an hour and then we reluctantly broke the news to our little addict that her *pappie* was gone for good. To make matters worse, we were too far away from any store to buy a replacement. She was devastated.

A DREAM BREAKS A BAD HABIT

I finally had enough. I took my upset angel out on the back deck so we could talk privately. I was hoping I could say something that would help to *get the monkey off her back*. I searched for words to soften the blow of my news: *I planned to end her obsession with pacifiers right then and there.* As we talked, my daughter clutched her three remaining pappies and cried as she listened to me. Then I had an idea, a stroke of wisdom. I looked at my precious girl and asked, "Is there anything you love more than your pappies?" I was sure she would say her greatest love was me or her mom, but that was not what came out of her mouth. Jenna thought for half a second, then looked me in the eyes and said, "Daddy, I love ballerinas more than I love my pappies." I was bewildered at first, but this actually made perfect sense. She often dressed up like a ballerina when she was playing. She had a ballerina music box and even had ballerinas gracing the wallpaper in her bedroom.

She said, "I love ballerinas so much, I want to be a ballerina." As I listened to my girl express her ballerina dreams, I saw a perfect opportunity to break her addiction. I told her I was going to do something very special for her when we got home from our trip. I said, *"When we get home, I am going to sign you up for ballerina classes. I am going to buy you a ballerina outfit and real ballerina shoes. There will be recitals and plays and we will all come to watch you. You are going to be a ballerina."* She was so excited that she hugged me, thanked me, and jumped up and down on the deck in joy over the prospect of getting to live out her fantasy.

Then I shifted the conversation. I made her look at me. *"Sweetheart, I am going to do this for you,"* I told her, *"but I need you to do something for me."* I told her that no ballerinas had pappies. *"If you want to be a ballerina, then you have to give me your pappies."* To my utter amazement, my young daughter handed her pacifiers to me without any struggle at all. The first night, she asked for them once; after that, she never asked again. With one solitary event, the addiction was broken. The nightmare was over.

PART OF A FATHER'S ROLE IS TO HELP HIS CHILDREN LET GO OF WHATEVER IS HOLDING THEM BACK BY OFFERING THEM SOMETHING GREATER THAN WHAT THEY HAVE.

Part of the role of a father is to help his children let go of whatever is holding them back. You do this by offering them something greater than what they have. Subtraction works best when it's paired with addition. What I did for my daughter on that deck was take away a lower identity and replace it with a higher calling. Her young mind was convinced that pacifiers were a necessary part of who she was. That thought was so strong that it fostered an addiction. But I helped her see something better. She was gifted with a dream for the future that was more powerful than what she depended on in the present. My baby girl graduated to another level when she handed me the things that represented her self-accepted label. When you have been shown the greater, it is easy to give up the lesser. This principle works for aspiring ballerinas—and it works for you and me.

I mentioned this incredible promise from our Father earlier, but it bears repeating: *"No eye has seen, no ear has heard, and no mind has imagined what God has prepared for those who love him"* (1 Corinthians 2:9). If you read this chapter in its full context, you will see that Paul is not writing about something way off in the distance, like heaven. He's writing about the wisdom of God and the power of the gospel that awakens us to the reality of what Jesus has done for us. He wanted the Corinthian church to drop its *pacifier* and go after the future God had for them. He knows they are immature and distracted by the false comforts of religion, so he offers them a bigger dream. If we will let Him, this is what our heavenly Father does for all of us. He offers us what our souls long for so we can lay down what is holding us back.

PEERING PAST DIRTY GLASS

A few years ago, I befriended a young family while I was waiting to board a delayed flight. We were all bored, so I struck up a conversation. This mom and dad had their beautiful six-month-old baby boy with them. We became fast friends. After a while, they let me hold the baby while we talked. I asked for their permission to show him the huge jet that was parked just outside the terminal window where we were sitting. I was trying to introduce the baby to the miracle of flight, but my attempt was not working. I could not get him to look past the grease stains on the glass. The accidental *abstract art* on the thick windows enthralled him. He could care less that one of the greatest inventions of all time was parked a few feet away. No matter how many times I tried, this six-month-old could not see past what was directly in front of him. A minor distraction prevented him from focusing his attention on anything beyond the window.

We have all been there. We all have *dirty windows* in our lives. Your perception can easily be impeded by the ordinary things that obstruct the view of your extraordinary future. I believe God wants to *hold you up to the glass* so you can see what He has for you. He whispers, *"You can't imagine what I have prepared for you."* Moving forward means you have to see past your many distractions. But how? How can we see past the dirty glass of our lives and embrace the marvelous things that God has prepared for us? God wants to expand your mind. He wants you to know there is no place beyond the reach of His power. To take the analogy a step further, *He wants to take you past the window and put you on the plane.* God wants you to go beyond beholding. He wants you to enter into the miracle of the life He has always intended you to have.

God unveils and applies the miraculous by the working of His Holy Spirit. It is the Spirit of God who reveals what God has for us. Paul wrote, *"It was to us that God revealed these things by his Spirit. For his Spirit searches out everything and shows us God's deep secrets"* (1 Corinthians 2:10). The Holy Spirit points past the *dirty glass* and says, "Look at what God has planned for you!" He urges us see to past our distractions and *get on board* with what God has done so we can go places we have never been. The Holy Spirit lets us in on what God is thinking.

How awesome is that? Who would not want to know *God's deep secrets?* I want to know what God has called me to do and what He is thinking concerning me. All of that knowledge is available to us with the Holy Spirit, who brings you to the *window* and shows you the wonders of God. He urges you to join Him on the *back deck* so you and your heavenly Father can talk about your future. God's Spirit wants to give you a dream so powerful that you willingly give up anything that keeps you from receiving it.

Paul gave the Corinthian church further insight into the workings of the Holy Spirit when he wrote:

> *No one can know a person's thoughts except that person's own spirit, and no one can know God's thoughts except God's own Spirit. And we have received God's Spirit (not the world's spirit), so we can know the wonderful things God has freely given us.* (1 Corinthians 2:11–12)

The Holy Spirit knows the thoughts of God because the Holy Spirit *is* God. The Holy Spirit knows our thoughts because *we were created by God and for God.* The Holy Spirit is always trying to build a bridge between God's thoughts and our thoughts. He longs for us to know what God is thinking. He wants to reveal to us *"the wonderful things God has freely given us."* Thinking is a more spiritual activity than most people realize. With the Holy Spirit's help, your thoughts are a high-level way of communicating with God.

If you have asked Jesus to be your Savior, then His Holy Spirit lives inside you. (See, for example, 1 Corinthians 3:16; Galatians 4:6.) Because you have the Holy Spirit in you, your thoughts are no longer ruled by *the world's spirit*. (See Romans 8:5.) God is thinking about *you* all the time. His thoughts are not thoughts of condemnation; they are thoughts of love and grace. He has dreams and visions concerning you. (See Jeremiah 29:11.)

SPENDING TIME WITH GOD

We can find out what God is thinking by spending time with Him, in His Word, and in His presence. The Holy Spirit in you enables you to sense God's presence and get close to Him. He makes the pages of the Bible come alive and helps you apply the truth to your life. The Holy Spirit wants you to commune with the very mind of God. God's thoughts have the power to change everything about who you *think* you are. His thoughts hold the keys that unlock the life He has always wanted you to have. Knowing what God is thinking changes everything.

GOD'S THOUGHTS HAVE THE POWER TO CHANGE EVERYTHING ABOUT WHO YOU *THINK* YOU ARE. THEY HOLD THE KEYS THAT UNLOCK THE LIFE HE HAS ALWAYS WANTED YOU TO HAVE.

Maybe all of this sounds too good to be true. After all, people who say God is *speaking* to them are crazy, right? And isn't it arrogant to think we can understand what God is thinking? Paul knew that the Corinthians would have these same feelings, so he boldly addressed their concerns:

Only those who are spiritual can understand what the Spirit means. Those who are spiritual can evaluate all things, but they themselves can-

not be evaluated by others. For, "Who can know the Lord's thoughts? Who knows enough to teach him?" But we understand these things, for we have the mind of Christ.   (1 Corinthians 2:14–16)

What a statement! We have *"the mind of Christ."* One translation says this means we are *"guided by His thoughts and purposes"* (AMP). In other words, we who are in Christ see past *the dirty glass* that has clouded and distracted the thinking of mankind. Having *the mind of Christ* means we have been spiritually gifted with the ability to process our lives in a new way. We get to know the *purposes of His heart*. We can know God's thoughts and His thoughts can change the way we think. We can think like Jesus. This kind of thinking will lead to a new life.

WONDERFUL WONDER

I used to think I was an introvert. I was a bit shy and I had a lot of social anxiety. Fear overpowered me whenever I engaged socially, especially in groups. This became a real problem as I entered the ministry. I tried to be relational, but it always felt awkward and unnatural. Eventually, I asked some trusted counselors for advice. I also devoured what the Bible says about relationships and anxiety. Eventually, I realized that my issue was my mentality, not my personality. I had allowed the self-imposed labels of my youth to give me an insecure mind-set as an adult. My tendency to be introverted did not mean I had to be a *loner*. I developed a habit of thinking differently about myself and my temperament. I asked God to reveal to me who I really was. With the help of the Holy Spirit, I faced my fears and pushed myself to be more and more socially active. Over time, my social anxiety was replaced by a genuine desire to connect and interact with others. Small changes in my thinking caused big changes in my life.

I believe we are meant to embrace our God-given personalities. I also believe we are never supposed to embrace our fears. There is nothing wrong with being introverted, but there's a lot wrong with living your life in fear. I used to coddle my anxiety because I erroneously believed it was part of who I was. I didn't believe I was gifted at being relational either. I was wrong on numerous levels. Over time, I developed social skills and thrived in both one-on-one and group settings. I embraced the wonderful truth that God wanted to bless me with relationships. Refusing to accept myself as just an *inward* person gave me an abundance of *outward* blessings.

I have come to cherish what David wrote in Psalm 139. It's a gift to anyone who ever struggled with self-love and a welcome interruption to those troubled by a pessimistic approach to their own personality:

> *You formed my inward parts; you covered [wove] me in my mother's womb. I will praise You, for I am fearfully and wonderfully made; marvelous are Your works, and that my soul knows very well.*
>
> (Psalm 139:13–14 NKJV)

In the recesses of our souls, we know we are *wonderfully made* by God. Everything God creates is perfect and wonderful. Have you mentally criticized His perfection? What have you thought about yourself that is less than wonderful? Today is the day to start thinking in a new way. If you fill your mind with Scriptures like Psalm 139, you will soon destroy your invalid patterns of thought and experience a life-altering attitude shift. Change begins in the mind.

~~~~~~~~

IF YOUR CONTEMPLATION OF YOURSELF CREATES NO *WONDER*, THEN YOU HAVE NOT DISCOVERED HOW WONDERFUL GOD THINKS YOU ARE.

~~~~~~~~

It is impossible to say the word *wonderful* without saying the word *wonder*. The Merriam-Webster online dictionary defines *wonder* as "a cause of astonishment or admiration," "the quality of exciting amazed admiration," and "rapt attention or astonishment at something awesomely mysterious or new to one's experience."[7] Its definitions of *wonderful* include "exciting wonder: marvelous, astonishing" and "unusually good: admirable."[8]

When you discover something *wonderful*, it creates unexpected and unfamiliar emotions. This is what God wants you to experience when you ponder *the wonder that is you!* If your contemplation of yourself creates no *wonder*, then you have not discovered how wonderful God thinks you are. You are His creation. God created you with a divine intentionality that has set you up for the specific future He has for you. This means you can embrace the *godly wonder* that is you, and let go of the limitations you and others have placed on your identity and your life. Just because several people have said something about you does not make it true. Just because you have always had detrimental feelings about yourself does not mean those feeling have power over you. Stop believing that the longevity of a label somehow gives it more authority. What God has said about you is timeless. You are wonderful because *you are His*.

FORMED BY THINKING HEARTS

Have you ever thought about the connection between the heart and the mind? Solomon did. In fact, he wrote that as a man *"thinks in his heart, so is he"* (Proverbs 23:7 NKJV). The idea that the heart can think is a big truth with massive ramifications. If you have a thinking problem, then you also have a heart issue. The mind and the heart are linked together. Jesus took this concept further when He said, *"Out of the heart proceed evil thoughts"* (Matthew 15:19 NKJV). A person cannot deal with the evil coming out of their mind without addressing the condition of their heart. Mentality is influenced by spirituality. The phrase *"so is he"* in Proverbs 23:7 is bursting with implication. *Thinking* is not only a dual event of the heart and mind, it's also a defining act of the soul. Your *thinking heart* ultimately forms your identity.

If we want to be who God wants us to be, it is essential that we *think from our hearts* how God wants us to think. We need to exchange our thoughts for God's thoughts. His way of thinking is better than ours.

---

7. www.merriam-webster.com/dictionary/wonder.
8. www.merriam-webster.com/dictionary/wonderful.

> *"My thoughts are nothing like your thoughts," says the* LORD. *"And my ways are far beyond anything you could imagine. For just as the heavens are higher than the earth, so my ways are higher than your ways and my thoughts higher than your thoughts."*   (Isaiah 55:8–9)

Note that God references His *thoughts* before He mentions His *ways*. Thoughts produce behavior. Our thoughts are not like His, therefore our ways are not like His. In these verses, God is provoking our curiosity about His heavenly thinking and divine ways. He loves it when we wonder what He's thinking. He loves it when we set our hearts on His thoughts. He knows if we think more like Him, we will be more like Him. If your thinking changes, everything else can change, too. Thinking begets being.

THINK TO YOURSELF

When my son Jordan was little, he loved to play with Legos. He would spread them out on the living room floor and meticulously construct whatever he was envisioning. Like most children, when he played, he constantly talked to himself, chattering on about his creative ideas toward his imaginary structure. The conversations he had with himself guided him as he ordered his make-believe world. This *internal dialogue* is one of the ways children form their personalities and their sense of self. They mentally process the information they are receiving from their environment and their internal dialogue spills out when they play. When the child is speaking positive words aloud, you know something good is happening in their heads. Conversely, negative verbalization is a sign that something is wrong. The same is true for all of us.

Have you ever been around a *fast talker?* I certainly have. Some people can mesmerize you with the rapid vocalization of their words. But the pace at which someone talks is *nothing* compared to how fast they can think. Research indicates that our inner speech—our thoughts—can function at a rate as high as four thousand words a minute, or ten times the pace of even the fastest talkers.[9] This means you and I can process information in our heads much faster than we can speak.

---

9. Rodney J. Korba, "The Rate of Inner Speech," *Perceptual and Motor Skills*, December 1, 1990; abstract accessed at journals.sagepub.com/doi/abs/10.2466/pms.1990.71.3.1043.

When you are thinking, you're not bound by the *rules* of speech, nor do you need your breath, voice box, or tongue. In your private cognitive conversations, you never have to stop and explain to yourself what you mean. When you mentally process, tone of voice and facial expressions cease to matter. Body language is irrelevant because your thoughts could care less about it. Thinking is by far the most efficient way to communicate information to yourself. It's also the fastest way for you to change.

To illustrate, let's talk about driving fast cars. (I must warn you that everything I know about this subject comes from movies.) My *movie-based research* has shown me that the coolest thing you can have on your fast car is something called a *nitrous button*. You press it and nitrous oxide mixes with your fuel so you go *way faster* than your competition. Thinking in the right way is like installing a *nitrous button* in your mind. After all, whether we realize it or not, thinking is like a high-speed race for a high-stakes prize. He who thinks the best wins. The one who consistently thinks like Jesus never stops winning.

When you intentionally think like God wants you to think, you are pressing the *nitrous button* of change in your life. This level of thinking is a godly mix that rapidly speeds up the process of becoming the person God has intended you to be. When the conversation inside of your head—your internal dialogue—starts to line up with what God has said about you, you better tighten your seatbelt because swift progress is about to be made. Godly thinking ejects the *old you* from the driver's seat. You now have new directions and new destinations. A better way of thinking races you toward the life God intends for you to have.

In his letter to the Ephesians, Paul wrote about a war between two ways of thinking. One way produces confusion while the other produces hope.

> *With the Lord's authority I say this: Live no longer as the Gentiles do, for they are hopelessly confused. Their minds are full of darkness; they wander far from the life God gives because they have closed their minds and hardened their hearts against him.* (Ephesians 4:17–18)

A confused mind leads people toward hopelessness, darkness, and hard hearts, taking them away from the life God wants them to have. In the case of the Gentiles mentioned here, they have hung a *closed for business* sign on their foreheads. Their minds are made up. They do not want to think God's thoughts. By making this choice, they are defrauding their lives of hope. They forfeit the life He intended them to have.

The concepts we are talking about in this chapter are everywhere in Scripture. Right thinking is the *hidden in plain sight* principle of the Bible, the foundational activity for the life you are destined to live. Why do we miss it? Why is there such a resistance to the obvious? The problem is that our equation for change is backwards. We think *a better life equals a better mentality*. This is a powerful falsehood because it's partially true. A better life does positively impact one's mental state, but circumstantial improvement is an unreliable source for lasting attitudinal change. The condition of your life is *always* in flux, so how can changing circumstances lead to lasting change in *you*? The proper equation is *a better mentality equals a better life*. When the order is right, the change is sustainable. Lasting change is possible when we allow our spirituality to transform our psychology. Change begins and ends in the mind.

PERSONAL BRAIN SURGERY

"It's not like it's brain surgery." Over the years, I have passionately said this to my kids. When I'm trying to lower their fear about a new task, it's my go-to dad mantra. Granted, this is probably not a very motivating or effective method of encouragement, both because it is condescending and just plain wrong. The truth is, all learning is a form of *brain surgery*. We are demanding that our brains develop a new pattern of thinking and asking our mind to grasp a skill it did not previously possess. We are forcing ourselves to unlearn a fear and replace it with a new confidence. When we teach ourselves an unfamiliar pattern of thinking, we are, in a sense, performing *personal brain surgery*. Even illustratively speaking, that's a big statement, so let me explain.

Over the past couple of years, I have been reading about neuroscience. It's absolutely fascinating! In my study and by personal experience, I have come to believe that our spirituality determines much of our neurology—that is, how a brain functions. Think about that for a moment. You are not simply a product of how your brain is wired. Your neurology (how your brain functions) does not have the final say over your spirituality (who you really are). Instead, spiritual change will change the way you think and that in turn changes your brain itself. In stating this, I am positioning your spirituality above your biology, placing God above your genetics. A godly transformation can override the negative effects of cultural influence. How you were raised and your life experiences thus far have no bearing on whether God gives you a new mind and a new life. You *can* change and your brain can change with you. Old destructive thought cycles can be broken and new healthy thinking habits can be put in charge of your mentality. Your brain does not have to be ruled by thoughts of the past. *You can change your mind.*

One of my favorite authors on this subject is Dr. Caroline Leaf. She has worked in the area of cognitive neuroscience since 1985. She is also a dedicated Christ follower. In her brilliant book, *Switch on your Brain*, she writes, "It was only a few decades ago that scientists considered the brain to be a fixed and hardwired machine. This view saw the damaged brain as incurable."[10] In other words, scientists believed the hopeless sentiment that once a pattern of thinking was established in your brain, it was irreversible.

In his wonderful book, *Rewire Your Brain*, Dr. John B. Arden writes:

Not long ago it was thought that the brain you were born with was the brain you would die with and that the brain cells you had at birth were the maximum number you would ever possess. The brain was thought to be hardwired to function in predetermined ways. It turns out that this is not true. The brain is not hardwired; it's "soft-wired" by experience.... Your brain is changing all the time.[11]

10. Dr. Caroline Leaf, *Switch on your Brain: The Key to Peak Happiness, Thinking, and Health* (Grand Rapids, MI: Baker Books, 2017).
11. John B. Arden, Ph.D., *Rewire Your Brain: Think Your Way to a Better Life* (Hoboken, NJ: John Wiley & Sons, 2010).

Both of these authors are promoters of a relatively new brain science called neuroplasticity, or the ability of the brain to change—to rewire itself—throughout your life. Your brain is not *set* in its function or patterns. Your brain can change for the better. This thinking is a hope-filled breakthrough...but it is nothing new to those of us who believe what the Bible says. Science is starting to catch up with what God has said about you and your brain. Science is discovering that *you can change your mind.*

Two thousand years ago, Paul wrote, *"Don't copy the behavior and customs of this world, but let God transform you into a new person by* **changing the way you think***. Then you will learn to know God's will for you, which is good and pleasing and perfect"* (Romans 12:2). God always knew we could change our minds. When your mind is transformed, you become aware of the life God intends you have. You intuitively know what pleases Him, so you stop settling for less than the perfection of His will. A renewed mind causes you to be selective about what belongs in your thoughts and therefore in your life. Believers in Jesus have a spiritual mental standard that they can use to *test and approve* what is worthy of their time and energy. When the *pattern* of this world's way of thinking is broken, *routine* ways of living are interrupted. You have been given the power to think new thoughts and become a new person.

REPETITIVE GODLY THINKING

Change begins with a thought, but lasting change is about repetitive thinking. A single, godly thought can be like a rocket ship that takes you to new heights, but *repetitive godly thinking* continually fuels the rocket. Romans 12:2 says we are transformed by *renewing* our minds. This truth infers that mental and spiritual renewal are connected. One thought from God can instantly transform us, but it is the repeated thinking of godly thoughts over time that fully forms us.

The psalmist wrote:

Blessed is the man who walks not in the counsel of the wicked, nor stands in the way of sinners, nor sits in the seat of scoffers; but his de-

light is in the law of the LORD, *and on his law he meditates day and night.*   (Psalm 1:1–2 ESV)

This psalm is about a man who thinks and acts differently than the culture around him. He is blessed because he receives his *counsel* from God. *"In all that he does, he prospers"* (Psalm 1:3 ESV). The secret of his life was not found in a single thought, but in his continual reception of godly *counsel.* He meditates on God's law *day and night.* This guy has a healthy addiction to God's thoughts. He thinks about what God has said *all the time* and this has given him a *blessed* life, the life God meant for him to have. This can happen for all of us.

Dr. Leaf writes about how persistent thinking has the power to rewire our brains:

As we think, we change the physical nature of our brain. As we consciously direct our thinking, we can wire out toxic patterns of thinking and replace them with healthy thoughts. New thought networks grow. We increase intelligence and bring healing to our brains, minds and physical bodies.[12]

She is saying we can actually *wire out* our old-self dominated thoughts and reprogram ourselves over time. In another section of her book, Dr. Leaf writes, "Doing your own brain surgery or neuroplastic intervention of toxic thinking and renewing your mind is based on regular exercising of your brain; change takes place over time through continual persistence."[13] Thinking the way God wants you to think is like showing up at God's *mental gym* and giving your mind a workout. Your *neurological muscles* grow and you change in the best possible way. That is a workout we can all embrace! We are all capable of changing our minds.

Your brain is one of the Creator's most amazing gifts to you. But your brain is amoral—it can be used for good or for evil. Your thoughts can

12. Dr. Caroline Leaf, *Switch on your Brain.*
13. Ibid.

bless you or destroy you. Dr. Arden notes, "The brain weighs just three pounds, yet it's one of the most advanced organs in the body. It has a hundred billion nerve cells, called neurons, and many more support cells. That's equivalent to the number of stars in our galaxy."[14] God wants to use the wonderful power and productive mystery of your brain to bless you and others. What if you gave every cell and every neuron over to Him? What would He do with your marvelous mind if you put Him in charge of your thoughts? Your transformation would be just the beginning.

14. John B. Arden, *Rewire Your Brain*.

DISCOVERY QUESTIONS

What pacifiers do you need to drop to receive the future God has planned for you?

_____

_____

_____

_____

_____

What is the Holy Spirit speaking to you?

_____

_____

_____

_____

What are some negative patterns of thinking in your own thoughts?

_____

_____

_____

_____

How does a better mentality lead to a better life?

_____

_____

_____

_____

PART IV:

REDIRECTED

TEN

FEARLESS NAVIGATION

Jesus came and touched them, saying, "Rise, and have no fear."
—Matthew 17:7 (ESV)

A couple of years ago, I was contemplating a scary decision. I was trying to decide whether I would resign from the church I was pastoring and begin traveling as a full-time speaker. For some time, God had been prompting my heart in that direction. I was both terrified and excited by the possibilities. Jeanne and I planned a *prayer trip* where we would seek God and discuss what we should do. We both sensed that a change was coming and we wanted to be fully submitted to the Holy Spirit in every detail. On Sunday morning, we wanted to attend a church, but we had no idea where to go, so we simply googled the word *church*. We picked what looked like a good church that was close to our hotel, dressed up a bit, and headed to the service with an expectation that God would speak to us. That service ended up being a defining moment in our lives.

We walked into a wonderful, diverse church filled with kind people who greeted us with enthusiasm. We began to worship with the church as the Spirit of God was moving in our hearts. Every aspect of that morning encouraged us, but God especially spoke to me during one of the worship songs: "No Longer Slaves" by Bethel Music.[15] It was a tune I had heard many times and the chorus is inspiring: *"I'm no longer a slave to fear; I am a child of God."*

As I sang those words, God began to show me a mental image of myself. He revealed that my hesitation to resign from my church and go back on the road was based in fear. I know it sounds strange, but during that song, what I will call a *living picture* appeared in my mind. I could see a clear image of myself covered in dozens of *fish hooks* with fishing line attached to them. I noticed that any time the line on one of the hooks was pulled, I would fall off balance and start walking in a random direction. It was a weird image, but it spoke volumes to me. God whispered to my heart: "Those hooks are representations of your fears." Fears had embedded themselves in me. Now, fear was controlling me and pulling me off course.

THE CRUEL HOOKS OF FEAR

I've been fishing since I was a kid and one thing I know for sure is you cannot fish without a hook. If you haven't fished in a long time—or have never gone fishing—you might be surprised by how advanced hooks are now. Some modern hooks are actually sharpened by lasers. Some are chemically altered to provide a microscopic pointed edge that greatly increases the odds of a catch. These hooks are so sticky sharp that it takes very little effort to snag a fish. The *hooks of fear* inside me were so deceptively effective that I could not even remember them going in. Fear can be bold and arrogant, but it also can be subtle and cunning. Either way, once you are hooked by fear, your freedom of direction is compromised. Fear pulls you away from your destiny. It never leads you to the places you were meant to be.

It only takes a small hook to catch a huge fish. Fear hooks us with tiny lies whispered in the privacy of our minds. *You're not good enough.... If you try that, you will fail.... Nobody is going to support you.... How could God ever use **you**?* In a split second, you can receive or reject the lie. If you take the bait, then you are hooked and fear starts to reel you in. You can fight, but now, you're pulling against a force that wants to dominate you. Your

---

15. Bethel Music, "No Longer Slaves," on *We Will Not Be Shaken* (Bethel Music, 2015).

life is on the line. Your future has been compromised. The hooks of fear are sharp and they penetrate deep. You need help if you are ever going to be free again.

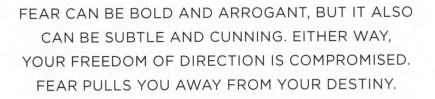

FEAR CAN BE BOLD AND ARROGANT, BUT IT ALSO CAN BE SUBTLE AND CUNNING. EITHER WAY, YOUR FREEDOM OF DIRECTION IS COMPROMISED. FEAR PULLS YOU AWAY FROM YOUR DESTINY.

We are given a battle cry in the letter to the Hebrews: *"God has said, 'I will never fail you. I will never abandon you'"* (Hebrews 13:5). Fear wants us to believe that we are left abandoned and alone. God wants us to know that He is always present. *"So we can say with confidence, 'The LORD is my helper, so I will have no fear. What can mere people do to me?'"* (Hebrews 13:6). You and I do not have to live in fearful hesitation. We can confidently obey God because He is always with us. Fearless living is possible, but only because our all-powerful God is present. The fear of what people will think about us fades as awareness of Him increases. Fear loses its influence when we understand that God is with us in every scary moment, surrounding us with His love.

When God revealed to me that I was *hooked* by fear, I instantly saw how it was affecting my choices. I needed to be free or I could never do what I was called to do. I asked God to remove all the fears embedded in me. In my mind and spirit, I could see the *hooks* dissolving and I saw myself being released from fear. I knew God had freed me from the force that was holding me back. By the end of that weekend, we decided to follow the leadership of the Holy Spirit and go on the road full time. Everything had changed. Fear was gone and our bold new direction was filled with faith and courage.

I discovered something powerful in the process of making that decision: you can follow the direction of your fear or you can follow the direction of your faith, but you cannot do both. Fear and faith pull in opposite directions. Fear causes us to be *off-balance* and makes our choices random instead of strategic. Faith causes directional assurance and creates peace in our hearts. Faith is stronger than fear.

SETTING SAIL INTO THE DEEP

Talking about faith always make me think of sailing. Like sailors, we people of faith need good navigational instruments if we are to survive in the vast open waters of our lives, where there are few points of reference. The further you venture out, the easier is to get lost or caught in a storm. Moving away from shore is never without risk, and it increases when you leave the protection of the harbor. Fear hates risk. Fear loves to lower our sails and addict us to the safety of the shallows. But when faith steers our ship, we can survey the *oceans of possibility* and follow the wind of the Spirit into the great unknown, where *"deep calls unto deep"* (Psalm 42:7 NKJV), with God as our compass and guide.

Chapters fourteen through sixteen in John's gospel are essential for anyone who wants to fearlessly follow Jesus. They include some of Christ's final recorded words before He was betrayed and ultimately crucified. In these passages, Jesus is preparing His disciples for the life He has divinely intended for them. At the beginning of John 14, we see two of the disciples, Thomas and Philip, struggling with their faith. Jesus wants them to see that all they are searching for is found in Him. Jesus implores Philip to *"at least believe because of the work you have seen me do"* (John 14:11). Then Jesus makes one of the most outrageous promises in the entire Bible: *"I tell you the truth, anyone who believes in me will do the same works I have done, and even greater works"* (John 14:12). In one mind-boggling statement, Jesus pulls the disciples far away from the safety of the shore. He invites them to sail into the terrifying *high seas* of faith, where anything is possible.

Jesus raised the dead. Jesus healed the sick. Jesus cast out demons and set the captive free. Jesus stood up to the powerful rulers of His day. Jesus fearlessly navigated His life through the treacherous waters of the culture He lived in. Now, these disciples—and you and I!—are promised that they—and we—can do *"even greater works."* What an astounding invitation from our Savior! This makes my fear cringe and my faith leap. This promise causes a *good* conflict inside of me that makes me want to give the Holy Spirit full control of my life. Jesus stirs the waters of His disciples' faith even further by telling them, *"You can ask for anything in my name, and I will do it, so that the Son can bring glory to the Father. Yes, ask me for anything in my name, and I will do it!"* (John 14:13–14). He is daring us to allow faith to overcome fear, beckoning us toward the vast seas we were always meant to sail.

In the next several verses of John 14, Jesus promises His disciples that He will send the Holy Spirit as their teacher, guide, and helper. Then He offers this calm assurance as a comfort to their overwhelmed minds: *"Peace I leave with you; my peace I give you. I do not give to you as the world gives. Do not let your hearts be troubled and do not be afraid"* (John 14:27 NIV). Jesus knows He is sending them into *turbulent seas.* He realizes He is telling them to *sail into a storm.* They could choose to let their fears keep them anchored in shallow waters by the shore, or they could follow Him and change the world. Jesus offers His peace as their companion as they travel into the unknown. I love that Jesus said, *"Do not **let** your hearts be troubled and do not be afraid."* This means we have a choice in the matter. We don't *have* to be afraid. We don't *need* to let our fickle hearts and our familiar fears direct our course.

ENTERING SCARY TERRITORY

When I was in my early twenties, I was a youth pastor in a small town an hour's drive from Kansas City. One of my first goals at that secluded church was to teach the students to love people outside of their own little world, so I began taking them to the inner city. Our youth group partnered with a church that was sharing the love of Jesus in some of the area's roughest neighborhoods. I loved the healthy *culture shock* my students experienced when they were exposed to these hurting places. I was proud of how they loved and served the amazing people we met on these excursions. Soon, I had requests from other youth pastors who wanted their students to be a part of what God was doing. We decided to create an annual mission trip to the city. Eventually, we had almost two hundred teens and adults participating. It was new territory for most of us, but it birthed in me a principle that I now live by: there is no limit to what God will do when we courageously follow His leadership wherever He wants us to go.

Those early days of ministry formed a foundation of willing obedience in me. I now have led or facilitated hundreds of mission trips and I founded a short-term mission trips organization called Partnership International.[16] I never tire of witnessing the transformation that takes place in someone who is willing to invest a portion of their life in an unfamiliar place. Life truly begins at the end of our comfort zones.

Last summer, I led a group of adults from Missouri to the beautiful country of Belize in Central America. Together, we finished the construction of a church in a Mayan village outside the capital city of Belmopan. The relationships we formed there will be something we will carry with us for the rest of our lives. Repeatedly, I heard team members talk about how the simple act of *going and giving* had changed them forever. Real life is about helping other people. This can and should happen in your own neighborhood, but sometimes, serving requires going to uncharted territory. To experience something you have never experienced before, you sometimes have to go someplace you have never been. The good stuff, the *God stuff*, is always found on the other side of your fears.

REAL LIFE IS ABOUT HELPING OTHER PEOPLE. THIS CAN AND SHOULD HAPPEN IN YOUR OWN NEIGHBORHOOD, BUT SOMETIMES, SERVING REQUIRES GOING TO UNCHARTED TERRITORY.

God wants to expand the territory of your life. He has plans to use you in places that are beyond the borders of your limited imagination. What you are familiar with is not all there is. God wants you to be open to new

16. pitrips.com.

possibilities of usefulness and influence. When Jesus set you free, He gave you a story that can be used to prompt others toward freedom. Can you see it? I can. I see you breaking out of your limitations and telling your freedom story to someone who needs to hear it. I see you bravely following the Holy Spirit past your fears and getting involved in causes that matter. I see God using your pain for a purpose. I see you living a life that could only be imagined in the mind of your Creator.

YOUR PERSONAL PROMISED LAND

In the first few books of the Bible, the life God destined His people to have is physically illustrated by the Promised Land, the land first promised to God's people through Abraham (see Genesis 15:18–21) and then to Jacob, Abraham's grandson (see Genesis 28:13). Located just east of the Jordan River, this bountiful land was ruled by fierce enemies of the Jewish people. It was not a place where Israel could just march in and take over. The Promised Land was filled with danger, but it was also filled with great prosperity and opportunity. It was theirs, but they had to show up and fight for it.

Instead, the Israelites refuse to fight, following their distractions instead of God's directions. They disobey God and are enslaved by the Egyptians for 430 years. (See Exodus 12:40–41.) Then God sends a deliverer, His servant Moses. Even in freedom, however, they wander away from their Promised Land, becoming lost in the wilderness for forty years because of their complaints, bad choices, and lack of faith. (See, for example, Numbers 14:34–35; Joshua 5:6.) God faithfully pulls His people toward the place He intends for them, but He does not force anyone into His purposes. The Israelites follow their lusts and their fears instead of following God. Eventually, led by Joshua, a new generation arises that is willing to obey God and follow His direction.

The people Joshua leads into the Promised Land are the grandchildren of the original slaves from Egypt. (See Joshua 5:4–7.) Many of them were born while the Israelites wandered in the wilderness. These chosen ones have a clear destiny, but they also have hundreds of years of slavery in their generational DNA, a built-in historical tendency toward bondage and fear. In the book of Joshua, we are told that this group makes it to the edge of the Promise Land, standing on the banks of the Jordan River. (See Joshua 3.) Excitement and fear equally permeate the atmosphere. When they cross the river, they will enter a new life—and they will face more enemies than they can count. God is telling them to go, but fear is begging them to stay. What they do next will determine the course of Israel for generations to come.

God always calls us to places that are contested territory. Fear wants the blessings without the battles, but that's not how destinies are realized. I addressed this earlier, but let me take it a step further: God's goal is not to push us along toward the life He plans for us, but to *transform us*. Our ultimate prize is to *become like Jesus* on the way to our divine destiny. God could easily clear the path, remove all struggles, and wipe out the enemies who possess *the land* He's promised us. That approach would only place *slaves* in a land meant for *warriors*. God loves us too much to grant us His *promised land* without saving us from ourselves. *Becoming* comes before blessing.

In Joshua 1, a new generation of Israelites is gathered near the Jordan River. God is about to take them into the Promised Land. But first, He reestablishes His promises to His people through their new leader, Joshua. Three times, He encourages Joshua, *"Be strong and courageous"* (Joshua 1:6; 1:9; 1:18). In the same way Jesus told His disciples He was always with them (see Matthew 28:20), God gives the Israelites the promise of His presence, saying, *"The LORD your God is with you wherever you go"* (Joshua 1:9). He promises them success and prosperity if they move forward with strength and courage. Joshua prepares the people by telling them that in three days, they will enter the land that God promised them so long ago. (See Joshua 1:11.) Can you imagine the palpable combination of anxiety and expectation they are feeling? Providential moments are always like this. Wherever you find great opportunity, you will also find great fear. Fear lives on the edges of promised lands and it will keep you from crossing into them if you let it. To enter what God has for you—your destiny—you must walk past your fear.

Two chapters later, we are given a front-row seat to history. The people approach the Jordan River, the last barrier that separates them from what God has for them. Joshua wants the priests who are carrying the ark of the covenant, which represents the presence of God, to go first. He wants to lead this expedition with a symbol that represents the source of their courage: the fact that God is with them. If you are unfamiliar with this story, you might be picturing the Jordan River as a lazy, shallow stream, but, in fact, it's at flood stage and overflowing its banks. (See Joshua 3:15.) The first time I read that passage, I thought, *Of course, the river is flooded—it has to be flooded.* Rivers are always flooded when we are about to enter new territory. Every godly conquest is preceded by a conflict. The current of fear is always raging in the waters that separate us from the life we are called to live. But if you have faith, something miraculous will happen, just as it did for Israel.

FEAR LIVES ON THE EDGES OF PROMISED LANDS AND IT WILL KEEP YOU FROM CROSSING INTO THEM IF YOU LET IT. TO ENTER WHAT GOD HAS FOR YOU—YOUR DESTINY—YOU MUST WALK PAST YOUR FEAR.

As soon as the feet of the priests who were carrying the Ark touched the water at the river's edge, the water above that point began backing up a great distance away.... And the water below that point flowed on to the Dead Sea until the riverbed was dry.　　(Joshua 3:15–16)

Do you see the *fearless faith principle* on display here? God makes them go past the edge and get their feet wet. Then and only then does He perform the miracle that removes the obstacle. Most of us never get near the edge of our destiny, let alone *wade into it.* We wait for God to move before we are willing to take a step. Unfortunately, that's not how faith works.

Faith heads for the river while the water is still raging…and steps into the flow. Faith demands a courage that's greater than logic.

> *The priests who were carrying the Ark of the LORD's Covenant stood on dry ground in the middle of the riverbed as the people passed by. They waited there until the whole nation of Israel had crossed the Jordan on dry ground.* (Joshua 3:17)

The leadership and obedience of a few opened a path for many. God never takes us anywhere for us alone. The new territory He is directing you toward will carve a trail for others to follow. When you fearlessly navigate your life toward what God is promising you, it will inspire others to do the same.

COURAGEOUS STAYING

My dad introduced me to hunting when I was eleven years old. One of my father's friends graciously hosted us in his home in central Illinois each year and allowed us to hunt on his farm. I can vividly recall my first cold, rude awakening at 4 a.m. on the opening day of deer season. I put on all of the clothes I had, including three pairs of socks, and tied on a pair of my dad's oversized boots. After I stumbled down the creaky stairs of that farmhouse, I forced myself to eat a hearty breakfast as I listened to the experienced hunters talk about the plans for the day. Then we all bundled up and ventured out into the frigid darkness. Until that morning, I had never been in place that was truly dark. In the city, light radiates everywhere you go. We walked deeper into the wilderness and the lights of the house faded until I could no longer see my hand in front of my face. I followed Dad's bouncing flashlight. I had no idea where we were going, but I knew adventure was waiting for us there.

We arrived at the base of a tree that had a ladder built into it. Dad told me this was the tree stand I would be hunting from. He helped me climb onto the small raised platform and gave me some basic instructions. After pointing into the darkness to show me what direction he was going, Dad climbed down and headed off. I watched his light bounce over the hill until I could no longer see it. I was alone in the middle of nowhere. I had never been to this place in daylight and now I was sitting there in the dark. Fear crept into me faster than the cold air. I tried to hold it together as my mind replayed every scary movie I had ever seen. Someone or something was going to get me.

Then it happened. If I had not been there, I would not believe it myself. Suddenly, I heard a loud shrilling sound like someone was screaming. It sounded like they were in the tree with me! I lost it. I started jamming shells into the gun Dad left with me—the same one he told me to wait until daylight to load. I wanted to run, but I had no idea where I would go. Plus, my father had ordered me to stay put. I had no explanation for what I had just heard, but I knew I could not leave the tree. I would fight, but I would not flee. I gripped my weapon and waited for daylight.

I found out later that screech owls are common in those woods. One of them must have roosted near the tree I was in and let out a defensive cry. A screech owl is the only thing in the woods that makes a noise like the one I heard…at least that's my theory. All I know is it took courage not to flee. Dad placed me in a spot that positioned me for opportunity. I just had to be brave enough to stay there. Later that morning, I shot a deer. Dad was proud of me and I was given the gift of a lifelong activity that I could someday pass down to my own son.

WHEN GOD CALLS SOMEONE TO A NEW LIFE, IT DOES NOT ALWAYS INVOLVE A RADICAL MOVE. SOMETIMES, GOD CALLS US TO SIMPLY STAY. OBEDIENCE MUST BE WILLING TO MOVE…OR WAIT.

I've thought about that first morning in the dark many times. What if I had responded to my irrational fears? What if I had climbed out of the tree and ran? I would have disappointed my father, put myself in danger, solidified my fear of the dark woods, and robbed myself of the opportunity that walked into my sights a few hours later. I could have cheated myself out of all future wilderness experiences. The courage to stay rewarded me beyond what I could comprehend.

When God calls someone to a new life, it does not always involve a radical move. Sometimes, God calls us to simply stay. Obedience must be willing to move…and obedience must be willing to wait. Maybe you feel like your life resembles a vast, dark wilderness filled with scary creatures. Maybe you wish you could run to a place where the opportunities may be greater. But God is present right where you are, your *"refuge and strength, always ready to help in times of trouble"* (Psalm 46:1). Where God is, anything is possible—and He is everywhere, *"in all the heavens and earth"* (Jeremiah 23:24). His blessing is found in obedience, not *movement*. You must love God enough to stay put or venture out at His prompting. God can bless you wherever you are.

The last words Jesus spoke before He ascended back into heaven are found in the Acts of the Apostles. He reaffirmed His promise to send the Holy Spirit and empower His church to accomplish their mission. He tells them, *"You will receive power and ability when the Holy Spirit comes upon you; and you will be My witnesses [to tell people about Me] both in Jerusalem and in all Judea, and Samaria, and even to the ends of the earth"* (Acts 1:8 AMP). Note the order of geography in this verse: Jerusalem was the apostles' city of residence, Judea and Samaria would represent a regional outreach, and then Jesus greatly expands their mission, sending them out to share the gospel with everyone on the planet. This commission includes every tribe, every language, and every culture. But note that Jesus tells them to start at home and branch out from there. The Holy Spirit would empower them right where they were and then He would send them to other places. He called them to *stay* before He called them to *go*.

Some exciting questions emerge from Acts 1:8. First, are you willing to obey God locally and regionally? The same call placed on the early church is placed on us. Second, are you so in love with Jesus that you would you would follow Him anywhere? The people in Acts would have to thrive where they were and then be willing to venture out. Finally, will you embrace both the adventure and the struggle of your faith? The call of God on our lives is not meant to be used as an escape clause from our personal realities or responsibilities. We must be willing to *bloom where we are planted* as well as *grow so we can go*. We cannot let fear tie us down or make us flee. We need to follow where Jesus leads us, moving when He moves and staying when He says we must.

All of this *stay or go* talk has prompted a caution in me. I want to be clear that you should *never* stay in a place where you are being harmed or abused. Sometimes, movement is necessary. Fearless navigation means you will do whatever you have to do so you can serve God to the fullest. If you are in a situation where you are in danger, do whatever it takes to get help. Everything we have talked about in this chapter requires the guidance of the Holy Spirit and the wisdom of God. Wisdom never leads us to stay in a place where the possibility to thrive is taken from us. Sometimes, you must leave the *tree stand* because real danger is there. If you are in a situation like this, I am praying for you. I pray for your protection and direction. I pray that you will have both the wisdom to know what to do and the courage to do it.

TIME TO SELL THE VAN

We once owned a terrible, old minivan. I hated that van. I failed to have it checked out before I bought it, so I didn't realize it was loaded with problems. By the time we became familiar with all the issues, it was too late. Among other problems, this minivan burned a quart of oil for every tank of gas. We had mechanics look at it and discovered the cost of repairs far exceeded the value of the vehicle. So we bought a case of oil and reluctantly decided to put up with all of the mechanical headaches. A few months later, we moved and became staff pastors at a church in Montana. The van made the trip, but its issues kept getting worse. We were in a bad position. Our primary mode of transportation was unreliable and we could not afford to do anything about it. I was forced to admit that purchasing this disaster on wheels was a huge mistake in judgment. I had to do something.

I remember driving away from yet another repair shop and yelling, "We have to sell this van!" I knew we would take a loss and we would have barely any money to put toward the next car. But maintaining this one was just a recipe for more frustration. I drove the van to a used car dealer instead of another mechanic. I was as honest as I could be and I ended up trading that nightmare for an even older car. There was nothing cool about my new ride, but it ran well and it was reliable. We drove that car, the product of our mistake, for the next three years. Sometimes, you have no choice—sometimes you must sell the van.

That van came into our lives because of my impatience and immaturity. I wanted something better for my family, but I was not willing to wait until we could afford it. I didn't remember to pray about buying the van before I wrote the check. It was a rushed purchase found on the Internet and I met the less-than-trustworthy seller under the lights of a Walgreens parking lot to complete the lopsided deal. How could I have been so foolish? My lack of discernment set our vehicle situation back several years. If only I had been patient. If only I had asked for advice. What I do know is this: the day I decided to sell the van, my situation began to recover. The road ahead was a long one, but at least we would not break down on it.

If you want to navigate your life in the direction that God is leading you, you need the right *vehicle*. God wants to provide you with a way to successfully get to where you are supposed to be. You can ill afford to drive around in the poor choices of yesterday. Stop paying the high prices of your worn-out methods of getting ahead. God wants to buckle you into His ways of advancing your life. His wisdom is the fuel your destiny demands.

My hasty van purchase screams of a lack of wisdom. Wisdom is not just knowledge. It's using knowledge to make sound judgments by understanding and acting upon what God says. Only the enlightening work of the Holy Spirit makes this kind of wisdom possible. Paul writes about this in his letter to the Colossian church:

> Be assured that from the first day we heard of you, we haven't stopped praying for you, asking God to give you wise minds and spirits attuned to his will, and so acquire a thorough understanding of the ways in which God works. (Colossians 1:9 MSG)

Our quick solutions are rarely in line with God's will for our lives. What we need is an *"understanding of the ways in which God works."* This requires us to reject the idea that we can run our lives by ourselves. We must be willing to *sell the van* when we make a mistake.

What situation are you in that requires a clean break? Is there an area of your life where you find yourself with no good options? Praying for a miracle is a great thing, but sometimes, the miracle comes in the form of wise direction. Sometimes, God refuses to *fix the van* and allows us to progress by urging us to stop and deal with our choices. Most people don't get out of debt overnight. No one loses a hundred pounds in a week. Relationships take time to heal. The important thing is moving forward, not your speed in getting there. *Selling the van* is not nearly as tough as being stranded because you refuse to acknowledge what needs to be done. Wisdom is quietly riding in your passenger seat and He is filled with hope. Hand Him the keys.

THE PRINCIPLE OF INDIRECT REWARDS

I'm a direct person, but getting right to the point can be a poor approach to relationships and an even poorer approach to life. Wisdom, especially from the Bible, often leads us in a roundabout way. Biblical wisdom is founded in a less-than-obvious principle we all need to understand. I call it *the principle of indirect rewards*. Biblically speaking, if you want to be blessed, you should not seek blessing—you should seek the God who blesses. In Deuteronomy, Moses tells the people of Israel to faithfully obey the voice of God and His commandments. He says, *"All these blessings shall come upon you and overtake you, if you obey the voice of the LORD your God"* (Deuteronomy 28:2 ESV). In other words, if Israel starts obeying God—chasing after God—the blessings of God would start chasing them. They would be *indirectly rewarded*. Most of us chase the wrong things. We are far too forceful and direct as we seek what God has for our lives.

The story of my old minivan is a good example. I should have sought wisdom, not a van. Wisdom would have led me to what I needed. Solomon wisely writes, *"The beginning of wisdom is this: Get wisdom. Though it cost all you have, get understanding"* (Proverbs 4:7 NIV). God wants us to prioritize wisdom in the order of our pursuits because it will lead us to His blessings.

Solomon also tells us, "*The one who gets wisdom loves life; the one who cherishes understanding will soon prosper*" (Proverbs 19:8 NIV). Prosperity is a byproduct of wisdom. This proverb enlightens us further:

> *Happy is the man who finds wisdom, and the man who gains understanding; for her proceeds are better than the profits of silver, and her gain than fine gold. She is more precious than rubies, and all the things you may desire cannot compare with her.* (Proverbs 3:13–15 NKJV)

I love that last phrase—"*all the things you may desire cannot compare with her.*" The rewards of wisdom are far greater than anything we could dream up for ourselves. Whatever it takes, we must get wisdom.

Wisdom is an antidote to fear. For instance, even at age eleven, if I had known about screech owls and their strange cries, I wouldn't have felt fear, no matter how dark it was. When I know what I'm doing, why I'm doing it, and the circumstances around me, fear dissipates. When I'm sure about a direction, I can navigate with confidence. Fear feeds on confusion and finds its home in disorientation, making us overcautious. Wisdom leads us forward, like an experienced guide on a wilderness adventure. God wants us to have wisdom and be fearless when He calls us to unfamiliar places.

I find it interesting that the Proverbs say, "*The fear of the LORD is the beginning of wisdom*" (Proverbs 9:10 NIV). In this entire chapter, I have taken a strong position against fear, yet here the Bible promotes a type of fear. What is this verse saying? The fear mentioned here is not advocating a fear-based relationship with God. Instead, it encourages us to have a holy reverence, an awe filled with respect for God. If you truly revere God, you make pleasing Him your life's priority. You long for His guidance because you know you can never *lead yourself* into the direction of His *divine intentions* for you. And, like all wisdom, the wisdom that comes from fearing God leads to great reward. Fearing God actually leads to fearlessness—because nothing else is greater or more powerful than Him. Fearing God leads to confidently following Him.

Do you need wisdom? Join the club! But all we need to do is ask for it. *"If any of you lacks wisdom, let him ask God, who gives generously to all without reproach, and it will be given him"* (James 1:5 ESV). God says He will generously pour His wisdom into us. You do not have to be the all-knowing navigator of your own destiny. All you really need is His wisdom! When you're wise, it takes less effort to get a far greater result. His wisdom will lift your weariness and get you to where you are supposed to be.

DISCOVERY QUESTIONS

What are some *hooks of fear* embedded in you?

_____

_____

_____

_____

_____

How does Jesus's promise of *greater works* affect your future?

_____

_____

_____

_____

_____

In what areas is God calling you to *stay or go?*

_____

_____

_____

_____

_____

How can you obtain greater wisdom from God?

_____

_____

_____

_____

_____

ELEVEN

GODLY GOALS

Commit your actions to the LORD, and your plans will succeed.
—Proverbs 16:3

I would like you to try a little experiment. Your assignment is simple: book a ticket to *nowhere*, as in *no place*. Yes, I'm asking you to book a trip without a destination. If you like, you can start by searching the Internet. Go to whatever website you prefer and type in your ambiguous destination. See how much it costs to travel to *nowhere*. I want you to travel in style, so go ahead and book a first-class seat...if you can. When you run out of options on the Internet, head to the counters at your local airport and see how many airlines are flying to nowhere. If you strike out there, try the bus or train stations. My suspicion is you might still be having a hard time, so expand your search. Maybe attempt to book a cabin on a cruise ship or hail a cab. If you try this exercise in futility, be prepared for a lot of rejection because I doubt anyone will be willing to assist you in getting to *nowhere*.

There are no flight plans to *who knows where*. Passengers don't board ships to sail out to sea without a port in mind. Roads and train tracks all lead someplace. A few cab drivers might take your money and just drive around, but even they will eventually insist that you tell them where you want to go. The truth is, no one can help you if you don't have a destination. The travel systems surrounding us are all designed for calculated movement to specific locations. Which is convenient because God has places for you to be. He has booked appointments for you and you should try to get to them on time. He has locations He wants you to experience and people He wants you to meet. The life God has designed you for is not a passive existence. It is never aimless or meaningless. God wants you to know where you're going. He wants you to have clear direction—and goals.

In his letter to the Philippians, Paul gives us insight into his life's ambition:

> *Dear brothers, I am still not all I should be, but I am bringing all my energies to bear on this one thing: forgetting the past and looking forward to what lies ahead, I strain to reach the end of the race and receive the prize for which God is calling us up to heaven because of what Christ Jesus did for us.* (Philippians 3:13–14 TLB)

Paul was a goal-oriented person. Throughout his ministry, to the last days of his life, he was driven toward a target set before him. Paul knew that a life well-lived for Christ included the pursuit of godly goals. The purpose of his life was neither puzzling nor pointless. Paul was always going somewhere to accomplish God's objectives for him. Paul was *a man on a mission*.

The ancient Greek philosopher Aristotle wrote:

> Virtuous activities or their opposites are what constitute happiness or the reverse.... The happy man...will be happy throughout his life; for always, or by preference to everything else, he will be engaged in virtuous action and contemplation, and he will bear the chances of life most nobly and altogether decorously.... If activities are, as we said, what gives life its character, no happy man can become miserable; for he will never do the acts that are hateful and mean. For the man who is truly good and wise, we think, bears

all the chances of life becomingly and always makes the best of circumstances.[17]

LIFE IS JUST BETTER WHEN WE HAVE *VIRTUOUS* GOALS, ESPECIALLY WHEN THEY ORIGINATE WITH GOD. GOD CREATED US TO ACCOMPLISH ASSIGNMENTS, EXECUTE HIS PLANS, AND FULFILL HIS *DIVINE INTENTIONS.*

I think Aristotle was right. Life is just better when we have *virtuous* goals, especially when they originate with God. God created us to accomplish assignments, execute His plans, and fulfill His *divine intentions.* The scriptural phrase *"God's will"* means that God has *willed* that we perform His ordained purposes. God wants to partner with us, through His Holy Spirit, to accomplish His strategic missions through us. He wants our lives to matter. When people see you and me, God wants them to think, *There is a person with a purpose, someone who is accomplishing something.* God wants the way we live for Him to motivate others toward their own divine purpose. God loves it when we have goals.

Proverbs 29:18 (MSG) says, *"If people can't see what God is doing, they stumble all over themselves; but when they attend to what he reveals, they are most blessed."* This speaks both to the consequences of chasing a vision-less life and the blessings that come from executing godly goals. If we fail to *"attend to what He reveals,"* we get off-balance. We literally *stumble all over ourselves* and get in our own way. But when we orient our lives toward the direction God reveals, we are promised His resources and power will enable us to finish the task. This promise is a wonderfully vast and invasive

17. Aristotle, *Nicomachean Ethics,* written in 350 B.C.; classics.mit.edu/Aristotle/ nicomachaen.1.i.html.

reality. God wants to help us execute many types of goals. Beyond the big goals for your future, God wants to inspire you to advance your character, your relationships, your professional life, your finances, and so much more. Another translation of Proverbs 29:18 says, *"Where there is no prophetic vision the people cast off restraint"* (esv). We all know people who have forsaken self-control because they have no vision or meaningful goals for their life. They are chasing everything except their destiny. When we lack strategic direction, our strength is wasted on worthless things. We need clear goals so we can live productive lives.

FINDING THE RIGHT WIND

I live in the barbecue capital of the world. Here in Kansas City, I am surrounded by more than 150 restaurants that are famous for their smoked meats. I have dined at many of them and they are all good, but one stands out: Gates Bar-B-Q. They are famous for their food—and their impatience with indecisiveness. The workers at Gates Bar-B-Q hate it when you can't decide what you want. When you are in line at Gates, you had better study the menu because when you arrive at the counter, they will quickly demand that you place your order. If you are indecisive, the waitress will be loud and adorably rude. She will move right past you to someone who is ready to tell her what they want. I get nervous every time I go there. I find myself practicing my order in the car and on my way into the restaurant. I don't want to blow it. I want to be decisive. (I think I just decided that I'm hungry!)

Like Gates, indecisiveness is on my personal hit list of things I detest. There is nothing worse than waiting in line to order your favorite food, only to be stalled by an unprepared customer in front of you. Indecision keeps you starving when you should be feasting. This is true of barbecue and it's true in life. Decision-makers advance to the head of the line. In a spiritual sense, they get to consume the good things God has for them because they know how to intentionally move forward. I get frustrated when I watch someone live a life of hesitation. I know God is directing them, but they are forever contemplating and can't commit themselves. Everything on the *menu* is good, but they refuse to place an order. Their inability to select a path becomes its own barrier, standing in the way of the life they were meant to have. Indecision is really a form of doubt. Doubt keeps us *forever deciding* and will rule our lives if we let it. God wants us to be free of doubt and hesitation. He is in the business of helping people make great choices.

GOD WANTS US TO BE FREE OF DOUBT AND HESITATION. HE IS IN THE BUSINESS OF HELPING PEOPLE MAKE GREAT CHOICES.

The Roman philosopher and statesman Lucius Seneca once wrote something profound about indecision. He said, "Our plans miscarry because they have no aim. When a man does not know what harbor he is making for, no wind is the right wind."[18] Maybe this is where you find yourself today. *"No wind is the right wind"* for you. No clear target has been established, so your *plans* are forever missing their mark.

What's the solution? How can you finally *plot a course and set sail* to reach the goals God has established for your life? The Bible tells us, *"Commit to the Lord whatever you do, and he will establish your plans"* (Proverbs 16:3 NIV). The first thing we must do is commit everything to God, placing our lives and decisions in His hands. Rather than vacillating back and forth, when we seek Him, He *establishes our plans.* This kind of behavior takes the pressure of accomplishment off of us and places it on Him, where it belongs. God promises to move you from *forever deciding* to *actively executing,* giving you direction and making your journey successful.

The only way to know whether an urge to do something comes from God is to develop a relationship with the Holy Spirit. Only the Spirit can show us what God intends for us to pursue. With the help of Scripture and the guidance of the Holy Spirit, you pray about your plans and reach a decisive conclusion about God's direction for your life. When you know that

18. Lucius Annaeus Seneca, *The Complete Moral Letters to Lucilius,* from Letter LXXI "On the Supreme Good," translated by Richard M. Gummere, Ph.D.; www.docdroid.net/ SpwJztN/seneca-moral-letters-to-lucilius-v8.pdf.

the direction you have chosen is in alignment with God's will, then and only then should an ambition become a goal. This process takes time and should involve the wise counsel of other godly people. In my experience, when God wants a direction for me, He often confirms it several times in several different ways. God does not want His plans to be a mystery you cannot solve. He longs to reveal what He has for you.

When you have both a clear direction and a sense of mandated purpose, you enter into what I call the *living goal stage*. At this point, you should write down your goals, giving a physical representation to the spiritual ideas inside you. I can remember times when I did this on the back of a napkin or a scrap of paper from an old gas bill. As God poured direction in me, I just had to give it immediate life. Later, I would clean it up and write it someplace more permanent. This action made things more real and engaged my senses on a much deeper level.

Recent research by Professor Gail Matthews of the Dominican University of California shows that writing down goals and sharing them with a friend makes you nearly twice as likely to achieve them.[19] Under the heading "The Righteous Shall Live by His Faith," the *English Standard Bible* says God spoke these words to the prophet Habakkuk: "*Write the vision; make it plain on tablets, so he may run who reads it*" (Habakkuk 2:2 ESV). Another translation puts it this way: "*Write my answer on a billboard, large and clear, so that anyone can read it at a glance and rush to tell the others*" (TLB). Notice that this is not a suggestion. God tells Habakkuk to *write* the vision and make the letters huge, so it's easy to read.

God wants us to be able to clearly see the vision He has placed on our lives. When we can see it, it is easier to *be it*. In my mind, I can see you buying a journal or downloading an app and practicing this skill. I see God meeting you as you write or type. I see a dry-erase board in an office that has God-given dreams written all over it. I see you motivated and accomplishing your goals.

---

19. Marla Tabaka, "New Study Says This Simple Step Will Increase the Odds of Achieving Your Goals (Substantially)," *Inc.* magazine, January 28, 2019; www.inc.com/marla-tabaka/this-study-found-1-simple-step-to-practically-guarantee-youll-achieve-your-goals-for-real.html.

Earlier, I mentioned the importance of obtaining godly counsel. We find the *right winds* for our lives, confirming what God has said to us, by receiving the wise thoughts of others. Solomon wrote, *"Without counsel, plans go awry, but in the multitude of counselors they are established"* (Proverbs 15:22 NKJV). Seeking godly counsel is a great way to obtain wisdom and conviction for the journey ahead. My advice here is *reach up*—pursue counselors who are ahead of you, spiritually wise and experienced. Seek people who know you because they are familiar with your strengths and weaknesses. Let them ask you hard questions and be vulnerable with your answers. Goals that are from God will always *weather the storm* of wise evaluation. Seeking counsel is an obedient act that will bring a blessing upon your dreams. Solomon said, *"For lack of guidance a nation falls, but victory is won through many advisers"* (Proverbs 11:14 NIV). Seeking counsel is a well-worn path to victory.

SPIRITUAL CPR

About fifteen years ago, I was asked if I would be interested in an open ministry position. At the time, I was traveling full-time as a speaker and had no interest in other pursuits. Then I was informed that the position would allow my weekends to be open so I could still travel to speak at churches and conferences. This position could expand my ministry without negatively affecting what I was already doing. I decided to do what I always do when I'm faced with a big decision: I prayed about it. In fact, I prayed about it a lot. As I prayed, I started to have an inkling of desire for this new position. My desire for the opportunity went from none to some. So, I talked with Jeanne about the possibilities and that conversation caused my desire to grow even more. I spoke with trusted friends and the desire expanded even further. I prayed and thought excessively about the various aspects of this opening. The desire to explore this further grew at a steady pace. Eventually, I had prayed and considered this opportunity so much that I was very interested.

The scenario I just shared with you is something I refer to as *spiritual CPR*. Think of it this way: when I got the call to interview for the job, my desire had no *heartbeat*. There was no *life* in the opportunity for me because I was not interested. So, I started performing *chest compressions* on the opportunity with my prayers, my obsessive thoughts, and my conversations with family and friends. The *heart began to beat.* The opportunity came alive. At first, it was dead as a doornail to me, but after obsessing over it, it appeared to be a living and breathing possibility for my future. Now I had to test it. *Was this opportunity really alive or was I breathing life into it?* I had to know whether I was talking myself into something...or if God was moving me toward it. I had to see if it would *live on its own.*

I've been in this position many times. I've processed opportunities so much that I can no longer tell the difference between what I want and what God wants for me. Am I enthralled with an opportunity or is God growing a pure desire in me? So, I developed a way to test whether my desires line up with God's purposes. It will sound strange, but when I find myself in a place of *spiritual confusion*, I simply stop praying about it, thinking about it, and talking about it. I go *cold turkey* with my obsession and let go of the opportunity. Every time it comes up in my mind, I just worship Jesus and give the whole thing to Him. I become *spiritually neutral* about the opportunity. This is a vital practice because I need to know whether it's God's will for me or not. *If I stop performing spiritual CPR, will the heart beat without my help?* Is there real *life* for me in this proposed direction or not? Is God in it...or is this just me?

In this particular case, without my help, the desire quickly decreased. When I started worshipping Jesus instead of begging Him for direction, the motivation in me toward the opportunity faded away. Soon, I was back to virtually no interest in the offer. My submission ended my obsession. Not long after that, I heard someone else had been hired for the job. Desire for this direction would not *live* on its own. The opportunity was not God's plan for me. I have experienced the opposite effects many times when praying (or not praying) about a new possibility for my future. When God wants something for me, it stays alive in me whether I obsessively focus on it or not. I pray and I seek counsel. I consider every perspective related to the opportunity. But if it is from God, I do not have to continue *spiritual CPR* to keep it alive. God's goals for my life do not require my obsession to obtain His confirmation. This whole process is about submission to God. I only want what He wants for me.

DELIGHTFUL DESIRE

If you want to know God's plans for your life, you should pay attention to your desires. Awareness of godly desire is an effective way to confirm godly goals. This is a principle and tool that I have used over the decades to help decipher God's will in my life. For example, a few decades ago, I attended a youth camp as a youth pastor. I brought a large group of students to this week-long event and they heard inspirational messages from a traveling speaker. Each evening, I struggled during the sermon part of the services. I could see myself doing what the speaker was doing. I had no jealousy or envy, but I knew God had called me to do the same thing. Finally, on the last night of that camp, I got alone with God and started criticizing my own desires. I *repented* to God for not being content and for being so ambitious. I questioned my own heart. That night, however, God spoke clearly to my spirit. He whispered, *"Son, I would have corrected that desire a long time ago if it was not from Me. I put that in you. The timing is not quite right, but the desire is from Me."* I patiently waited another year and then God launched me into a new ministry. My godly desire became a God-driven reality.

The psalmist says, *"Take delight in the* Lord, *and he will give you your heart's desires"* (Psalm 37:4). This is a wonderful verse that contains a power-packed promise, but it requires the right approach to avoid an obvious abuse of its truth. When we *"take delight in the Lord,"* we find pleasure by spending time with Him. As we do, He starts developing His desires in us. This verse does not say you can have *whatever your heart desires*. Rather, it is saying that God works in the realm of desire. When you delight yourself in the Lord, your desires and direction change. Rather than focusing on getting what you *think* you want, you start wanting what God wants for you.

Paul addressed the topic of desire with the Philippian church when he wrote, *"Work hard to show the results of your salvation, obeying God with deep reverence and fear. For God is working in you, giving you the* **desire** *and the* **power** *to do what pleases him"* (Philippians 2:12–13). Note that last part: it's God *"working in you"* who gives you *"the desire and the power"* to live out His purpose for your life. God always empowers what He inspires. Your ability to accomplish God's purposes dramatically increases when your desires are in line with what He wants for you. Look at it this way: it's far easier to accomplish something when the *want to* is in you. What would your life look like if *your wants* lined up with *God's desires?* Nothing would be impossible! Destiny-driven motivation explodes when God transforms your desires to match His.

GOD ALWAYS EMPOWERS WHAT HE INSPIRES. YOUR ABILITY TO ACCOMPLISH GOD'S PURPOSES DRAMATICALLY INCREASES WHEN YOUR DESIRES ARE IN LINE WITH WHAT HE WANTS FOR YOU.

Have you tested your desires with prayer and counsel? Have you compared them with His Word? Have you given your desires back to Jesus? Is the *heartbeat* of what you think God wants for you *beating on its own?* Do you have a God-honoring dream that will not go away? If your answer to these questions is *yes*, then your desires just might be in line with what God has planned for you. God loves it when you want what He wants!

Keep in mind, there are times when you need to be patient. The answers don't always come quickly. It can feel like it's taking forever for godly desire to cultivate in you. Being sensitive to divine direction is a learned skill. You will not naturally develop God-inspired goals without supernatural help. The good news is, God promises to reveal His plans to anyone who seeks Him.

POWERFUL PLANS

Plans always make me think of action movies. The scene is predictably the same: the ship is sinking... the plane is going to crash... the terrorists are going to kill everyone... Then a hero appears, a hero with a *plan*. Immediately, there is hope. We might not survive, but now, we have a chance. In my mind, the buff action star never shines as bright as when he has a beautiful plan. Nothing produces hope like a plan. When I have a plan, I'm naturally energized. Plans mean that a problem is about to be attacked. They create a clear direction that causes movement. Great plans make great movies—and great lives.

Simply put, a plan is the strategy behind a goal. Goals are broad and optimistic while plans are specific and realistic. Plans are necessary to navigate the real-time process of living out our goals. A plan may seem less exciting than a goal, until you consider that God does not just *set our course*, He also *gets in the boat* with us. God is present in both the revelation and the execution. God gives us goals and He meets us in our plans. Addressing plans, the Bible says, *"We plan the way we want to live, but only GOD makes us able to live it"* (Proverbs 16:9 MSG). God is all for planning, but He's against people who plan without leaning on His power.

Have you ever known someone who is *all talk*, all commotion but no motion? They have plans, but there's no resolve behind them. Paul gets it right when he says, *"The Kingdom of God is not just a lot of talk; it is living by God's power"* (1 Corinthians 4:20). Another translation succinctly says, *"For the kingdom of God is not a matter of talk but of power"* (NIV). The way of God is a way of power, not talk. We have done enough talking about change; we need the power to change. The Bible tells us, *"Be strong in the Lord and in his mighty power"* (Ephesians 6:10). Big plans demand big power. Godly goals fully rely on God's power. We have to continually remind ourselves that on our own, we can't get the job done. We need His power to accomplish His plans.

The difference between a *doer* and a *talker* resembles the difference between a real superhero and someone who just wears the suit. *Suit-wearers* go to conventions to talk about their favorite superheroes, but they never actually *do* anything *super*. They have the image and platitudes, but no power and no plans. They are all dressed up, but they have no place to go. They are impersonators, not innovators. But in Christ, we can have real power and make a real difference in this world. Jesus rescued us so we could rescue others. Superpowers are wasted resources unless they are used to accomplish meaningful goals. Therefore, plans are important because planning leads to doing.

A want is not a goal. You may want thousands of things that would improve your life, but without goals, how will you get any of them? Maybe you *want* to lose weight, get out of debt, or start a new career. But *wanting* is not even in the same realm as a godly desire. Maybe that's what David meant when he wrote, *"The* Lord *is my shepherd; I shall not want"* (Psalm 23:1 nkjv). Perhaps all of our endless *wanting* is the problem. We need to take our *wants* and convert them into *goals* by developing and executing *plans*. If you are just talking, you're still just *wanting*, fantasizing about what you *could* do, but never following through. God has called you to do more than just dream about a different life. He has called you to wake up and live it.

JESUS RESCUED US SO WE COULD RESCUE OTHERS. SUPERPOWERS ARE WASTED RESOURCES UNLESS THEY ARE USED TO ACCOMPLISH MEANINGFUL GOALS. PLANNING LEADS TO DOING.

You may have to sacrifice—and that's hard when you merely *want* something. Excessive wanting has a way of draining a person of their patience. Wanting cares nothing for process, but it loves gratification. Wanting can be dangerous because it fosters a temptation to compromise. The writer of Proverbs gives us this warning: *"Good planning and hard work lead to prosperity, but hasty shortcuts lead to poverty"* (Proverbs 21:5). Shortcuts are the chosen path of a person who is driven by wanting. Godly desire is the opposite because it grows the attributes of Jesus within us. His desires help us to patiently *work the plan*. Remember, our goal is not just to succeed, but to become more like Jesus in the process. This is the beautiful by-product of living out godly goals.

The mistake most of us make when planning is that we tend to think in *leaps* when we should by thinking in *steps*. David understood this truth when he wrote, "*The LORD directs the steps of the godly. He delights in every detail of their lives*" (Psalm 37:23). Paul wrote, "*Since we live by the Spirit, let us keep in step with the Spirit*" (Galatians 5:25 NIV). We walk out our faith and accomplish our plans one step at a time. A godly plan is like a treasure map that will lead you to what you are destined to have. Resist the temptation to take shortcuts. Commit yourself to a daily application of the plans God gives you. God will meet you in the mundane. He is proud of you when you are faithful to the plan.

BEAUTIFUL BOUNDARIES

Many years ago, I saved up airline miles and took my wife to Oahu, Hawaii. We arrived in paradise without much of an agenda. We just wanted to spend our days exploring the amazing beauty of the island. Every day, we drove our rental car to wherever our hearts took us. One afternoon, we found ourselves near the North Shore at a gorgeous beach that's famous for its strong currents and giant waves. That delightful day, the ocean churned and rolled as the inviting blue water beckoned us to get in. We played in the water like kids and had the time of our lives. We were even blessed by the presence of some large sea turtles that frolicked with us. Our afternoon at the North Shore gave us one of our best memories of our trip.

On the northern coastline of Oahu, the ocean currents and tides can easily carry you from place to place without your permission. You must be conscious of this or you can drift toward danger, or even swept out to sea. As we swam that day, we were keenly aware of the Pacific Ocean's vast power. At one point, in only few minutes' time, we were forced hundreds of yards from our original entry point. We fought our way back to where we started, only to be moved away again. After a while, I decided to establish some boundaries. There were some sunbathers down the beach from us, so I used them as a landmark. If we could stay between the towels we left on the beach and the sunbathers, we would be safe. Anything further and we could be in danger. We had to fight hard to stay where we belonged. But with the boundaries set, our fun continued all afternoon. Boundaries help to make the life you and I are called to live safe and attainable.

Life is filled with forces that can move you away from your goals. There are *riptides of temptation* that want to sweep you into pursuits and places you were never meant to seek. Without boundaries, you can easily lose track of your goals in the surrounding *sea* of unending possibilities. If you let yourself be tossed about by whatever *wave* comes your way, you will end up *drowning your dreams*. Plans are only as effective as you are intentional. Therefore, you must have boundaries. You are not called to everything, everyone, or everywhere. Just because there's a lot to do does not mean you are supposed to do it all. God has specific places for you to be and specific things for you to do. He chose your *stretch of beach* with great thought and care. Set boundaries that honor the goals God gives you.

When you say *yes* to God's plan for your life, you must also be ready to say *no* to anything that keeps you from what He has for you. You stay out of every *current* that leads you away from your destiny. There is power in your *yes* and protection in your *no*. Paul offered us some great wisdom when he wrote, "*No matter how many promises God has made, they are 'Yes' in Christ. And so through him the 'Amen' is spoken by us to the glory of God*" (2 Corinthians 1:20 NIV). Jesus has said *yes* to all He has promised you. So, you can say *amen*—so be it—to all He has said. You should be in agreement with God and line up your life with what He has called you to. Your powerful *yes* will create clear goals that lead to clear choices. Your *yes* to God's plans and purposes opens up new worlds, but it also creates new boundaries.

When I think about boundaries, I think about my Yorkshire Terrier, Kooper. He took full advantage of our large, fenced-in backyard during the first eight years of his life. It was his appointed territory and he ruled his outdoor kingdom with all the strength and joy his little body could muster. Squirrels and rabbits were the enemies; every smelly tree and smooth blade of grass were his friends. His daily routine was to survey every inch of the perimeter that surrounded his space. My dog loved that yard. If only we had not moved....

Our new house has a much larger yard. In fact, our yard connects to our neighbors' yards on both sides and a large, city-owned field in the back. But there's no fence. At first, we thought Kooper would love the vast freedom, but we were wrong. We now have to watch him when he goes outside and yell from the deck when he goes past our property lines. There are dangers and distractions everywhere. A lack of boundaries means there is less freedom, not more.

The psalmist says, *"God's laws are perfect. They protect us, make us wise, and give us joy and light"* (Psalm 19:7–8 TLB). Three verses later, we're told God's laws *"warn us away from harm and give success to those who obey them"* (Psalm 19:11 TLB). *God's laws* could be described as His *boundaries.* They are the scriptural warnings and restraints that both protect us and give us wisdom and joy. The boundaries of the Bible keep us from the insanity of self-sabotage, providing a light in the darkness and freedom in an ocean filled equally with pleasures and perils. In short, they keep us from hurting ourselves. God's *no's* complement His plans by ensuring that we live out His *yes's* and have both safety and freedom. With David, we can cry out, *"The boundary lines have fallen for me in pleasant places"* (Psalm 16:6 NIV). The Bible's restrictions are not designed to limit you or hold you back. Rather, His loving boundaries maximize your liberty while leading you to your destiny. Within these *borders*, you get to become all that He has made you to be.

DON'T FORGET TO FLY THE PLANE

One of the most avoidable plane crashes of all time occurred at 11:42 p.m. on December 29, 1972. Eastern Airlines Flight 401 was making a routine trip from the John F. Kennedy International Airport in New York to Miami International Airport. Everything was going according to plan until the pilots began their approach and lowered the landing gear. The captain noticed that the gear's indicator light was not working. Eventually, the entire flight crew was preoccupied with fixing the burnt-out bulb. They failed to realize that the autopilot function was inadvertently turned off and the plane was gradually losing altitude. The plane crashed in the Florida Everglades, killing 99 of the 176 passengers and crew on board that night. Two additional persons died later from their injuries. The National Transportation Safety Board report said, "Preoccupation with a malfunction in the nose landing gear position indicating system distracted the crew's attention from the instruments and allowed the descent to go unnoticed."[20] They inadvertently ignored the most important rule of flying: *don't forget to fly the plane.*

Most people are leading distracted lives. They are off-course, not looking at what God has placed in front of them. They have forgotten to *fly the plane.* The Bible encourages us to *"Look straight ahead, and fix your eyes on what lies before you. Mark out a straight path for your feet; stay on the safe path. Don't get sidetracked; keep your feet from following evil"* (Proverbs 4:25–27). God gives us goals so we can get to where He intends us to be. Those goals are the *flight plans* of our lives. If we are sidetracked with lesser things when we should be soaring toward our goals, we will soon head toward disappointment and disaster.

The life God has divinely intended for you to have will only be realized one goal at a time. Each completion will lead you to another step in the journey. Every goal you accomplish will build your confidence, giving you greater energy and faith to move forward.

20. https://lessonslearned.faa.gov/L1011Everglades/Eastern%20401%20ntsb%20report.pdf.

DISCOVERY QUESTIONS

How has indecisiveness affected your life?

_____

_____

_____

_____

What is moving you away or toward godly goals?

_____

_____

_____

_____

What desires are developing in you as you read this book?

_____

_____

_____

_____

Why is it important to establish boundaries in life?

_____

_____

_____

_____

TWELVE

PURE POTENTIAL

Blessed are the pure in heart, for they shall see God.
—Matthew 5:8 (NKJV)

I can still remember the day it arrived. It was deep in the winter, February 1985, I think. It was something I looked forward to each year. In fact, my seventeen-year-old male mind was obsessed with the event. I could sense it was coming and then it magically appeared in our mailbox. Of course, I am talking about the annual release of the *Sports Illustrated* Swimsuit Issue. (What else could I be talking about?) In past years, as soon as it was possible, I would search through its pages with a gawkish delight. But this year was different. I was not the person I used to be. Four months earlier, I had accepted Christ as my Savior and my life was forever changed by His unbelievable grace. I was different...but some of my old patterns were still in their predictable cycle. I needed to change that. It was time for my habits to catch up with my transformation. I figured that would be a project for another day.

I was wrong.

When the glossy magazine filled with Photoshopped perfection arrived, I compulsively opened it. I was about to do what I had always done: ogle some gorgeous models wearing next to nothing. But in the first few moments, before the visual assault could completely overwhelm my senses, I heard God's Spirit speak to my heart with calm authority. He said, *"You cannot have **this** and what I have for you."* My spirit stood at attention, but my mind began to argue. A competing thought emerged: *I am a red-blooded, teenage guy. This is not wrong, it's normal.* My mental courtroom was in active defense mode for several more minutes. I was the attorney of my own case, defending something I wanted. I self-argued my point from every angle I could think of...and then there was silence. The Holy Spirit had declared His position with a single sentence. My volumes of dissent were not budging the boulder of truth that had been dropped on me. I knew I was wrong, but I was struggling to accept it.

TIME TO MAKE A CHOICE

At the time, there was no way I could have known the ramifications of this small but far-reaching personal battle. I was not aware of how much was on the line. God was offering me a life that could not be experienced if my self-centered desires controlled me. He was proposing a future for me beyond anything I could imagine for myself. His ultimatum was short and powerful: *"You cannot have this and what I have for you."* What He was proposing and what I wanted were in extreme opposition, like two roads leading in different directions. Looking back on it now, that moment reminds me of Joshua telling the Israelites that they could not serve God and the false gods of Egypt simultaneously. He laid it on the line: *"Choose for yourselves this day whom you will serve"* (Joshua 24:15 NKJV). It is impossible to serve what enslaved you and also live in the freedom God is offering you. You must choose.

Maybe your personal patterns of addiction are a lot deeper and more destructive than those of a young man struggling with adolescent lust. Perhaps the *package* that arrives in your mind's daily in-box is the deadly temptation of drugs or alcohol. It could be that your slavery to lustful behavior exists far beyond the fantasy-filled pages of a magazine or computer screen. Maybe you have been a thief, a compulsive liar, or worse. If you have lived out the sinful dreams this world offers, then you know what it is to be in bondage.

The good news is that *today is a new day*. You don't have to open the addiction package again. There is no obsession that's beyond the power of the freedom Jesus offers. The application of God's matchless grace can end your self-sabotaging tendencies. The changes will start small, but they *will* come and the ramifications will reach all the way into your destiny. *But you must choose.*

How many *Joshua 24 moments* pass us by without our recognition or obedience? How often are we presented with a seemingly minor compromise, failing to calculate the major impact it will have on our future? We try to hold on to the dangerous comforts of our dark past while we seek to embrace the bright new day God is calling us into. It just doesn't work. Paul reminds us that we are *"children of the light and of the day; we don't belong to darkness and night"* (1 Thessalonians 5:5). We embrace what we *belong to* by directing our lives into our God-given identities and destinies. *Children of the day* love the light because we can see where God wants us to go. Darkness only compromises our vision, making us stumble and lose our way. The conflict between light and darkness is real. Here's what John wrote about living in the light:

> *This is the message we heard from Jesus and now declare to you: God is light, and there is no darkness in him at all. So we are lying if we say we have fellowship with God but go on living in spiritual darkness; we are not practicing the truth. But if we are living in the light, as God is in the light, then we have fellowship with each other, and the blood of Jesus, his Son, cleanses us from all sin. If we claim we have no sin, we are only fooling ourselves and not living in the truth. But if we confess our sins to him, he is faithful and just to forgive our sins and to cleanse us from all wickedness.* (1 John 1:5–9)

To realize our Creator's divine intentions for us, we must forsake the darkness and join God in His light. God's light shines upon the darkness of all sin, giving human beings the possibility of escaping its evil grip by receiving His great love.

On that winter day in 1985, I made the only choice I could. Cheap gratification is *nothing* compared to the richness of what my Savior was offering. When the Holy Spirit told me, *"You cannot have this and what I have for you,"* that triggered a powerful, *holy curiosity* in my mind that overwhelmed my self-centered logic. I realized, *God has something for me! What is it?* Thank God, curiosity about the future led me to forgo the obvious and immediate base gratification of a sordid magazine. I know there are far greater sources of seduction, but this one was mine and it inspired lustful thoughts and habits in me. Instead, my heart filled with a hope that is far stronger than any temptation. I chose to live the life God intended me to have.

God is making the same offer to *you* today. He never directs us away from our past without pointing us toward our future.

The moment I decided to throw away that magazine, I discovered a divine connection. I found out that my destiny and my virtue are inseparable. I could not *have* what God wanted me to have unless I was willing to *be* who God wanted me to be. I could not compromise my character and experience my calling. Purity creates a pathway for the purposes of God. It catches God's attention, moves His heart, and opens doors. Your purity sets your potential.

PURITY CREATES A PATHWAY FOR THE PURPOSES OF GOD. IT CATCHES GOD'S ATTENTION, MOVES HIS HEART, AND OPENS DOORS.

Let's stop and pray right now about any bondages that are holding you back:

Dear Jesus, we agree together that You alone can break the cycle of sin that keeps me away from my destiny. I ask You to set me free. I ask for Your forgiveness and I pray for Your restoration. I need a new direction. I need to be awakened to my purpose. I need the potential of my future to be greater than the pull of my past. Break every addiction and create new godly patterns in my life. Guide me and display Your grace in and through me. In Your name, we pray. Amen. So be it.

DIVINE APPOINTMENTS

The other day, I was thanking God for the ministry opportunities I have been blessed with during the last thirty years. I've met some of the most wonderful people on earth and experienced the joy of speaking into their lives. I have developed rich friendships with leaders who I admire and feel so honored to know. My ministry destinations have included almost every state in our country and many foreign nations as well. I have been humbled to minister to thousands of people and facilitate hundreds of meaningful mission projects. Somehow, by God's amazing grace, my life has impacted the hurting and the poor. I am overwhelmed with gratitude for the favor God has placed on my life. I know that without purity, none of this would have happened. My purity and my promotion are connected—and this same principle applies to you.

Consider these words from the prophet Hanani: "*The eyes of the* LORD *search the whole earth in order to strengthen those whose hearts are fully committed to him*" (2 Chronicles 16:9). Other translations say God searches for those whose hearts are "*perfect toward him*" (TLB) or "*completely His*" (AMP). God is constantly searching for the *pure in heart*. God blesses us when we develop our gifts and He loves it when we are courageous or creative, but what He *really* wants are people whose hearts are totally devoted to Him. Once He finds them, He promises to strengthen them. A blameless heart gets God's attention like nothing else. It makes Him stop searching and start blessing!

PREPARATION IS KEY

Imagine that you just booked an extremely important appointment that's a few months away, a high-level meeting that will change your life and the lives of others—*forever*. You can hardly believe you're part of something so important! You cannot miss any details. You want to be prepared physically, so you'll eat right, exercise, and get plenty of rest. Perhaps you'll buy a new outfit for the occasion. You'll also prepare mentally by reading up on everything you need to know beforehand. You might even practice your social and conversational skills. But most importantly, you would want to be in a good place spiritually and emotionally. You would want to have a pure heart.

No wise person would go to a life-changing meeting without preparation. Can you imagine showing up unprepared for that big interview, that mega negotiation, or that once-in-a-lifetime opportunity? Do you see yourself walking into a high-level appointment without training yourself for a moment of that magnitude? Of course not. With this illustrative backdrop, let me share a big truth that has matured me and expanded me over the decades: *the battles of life are won before they take place.* The war is won before the first shots are fired. The contest is decided before it begins.

~~~~~~~~~~

PREPARATION IS WHERE WE WIN OR LOSE THE BATTLES OF OUR LIVES. GOD READIES OUR HEARTS FOR BIG MOMENTS BY PURIFYING THEM IN THE PRELUDE.

~~~~~~~~~~

Preparation is where we win or lose the battles of our lives. It's the most crucial part of providence. God readies our hearts for big moments by purifying them in the prelude. He finds us in the lonely days of our existence and tells us we must get ready. His purposes are carried by prepared vessels. It is purity that sets up destiny.

A premier example of the importance of purity as part of the preparation for divine appointments is the life story of David. The Bible is full of David's many attributes and achievements, but the greatest accolade concerns the purity of his heart. David is called *a man after God's own heart*. (See 1 Samuel 13:14; Acts 13:22.) David is my favorite Bible character. What I love the most about his story is the fact that God chose David when he was unknown to everyone else. David was not from a notable family and he was the youngest of seven brothers. He was given a lowly, lonely job, taking care of the sheep. David was small and insignificant. In fact, when the prophet Samuel approached David's father, Jesse, to anoint one of his sons to be king, Jesse didn't even bother to call David in from the fields at first. Even his own father doubted him. But God saw something different in David. David was anointed to be king (see 1 Samuel 16:13) because God was drawn to the purity of David's heart. God saw a young man *whose heart was fully committed to Him* in the fields outside of Bethlehem. David's purity during his time of obscurity captured God's attention.

THE MUNDANE PREPARES US FOR THE
MIRACULOUS AND OUR PRIVATE PURITY
PREPARES US FOR PUBLIC PROMOTION.

David was faithful when no one else was watching as he protected his family's flock. I can just imagine him sitting among the sheep in the pasture, flinging stone after stone from his sling, unwittingly preparing for a divine appointment he knew nothing about. His faithfulness was tested in dramatic fashion when a lion and then a bear tried to attack the sheep. David managed to kill them both. These events stood out on David's resume when he *interviewed* with King Saul for the job of facing Goliath. (See 1 Samuel 17:34–37.) It turns out that shepherding prepared David for his destiny. He became a mighty warrior, killing a giant enemy with just a sling and a single stone. Who could have imagined that a shepherd's job was the training David needed to become the warrior he was meant to be? Only God.

The mundane prepares us for the miraculous and our private purity prepares us for public promotion. Like David, most of us are unaware of the opportunities we are training for. The fullness of God's plan has not been revealed to us. We do not have access to God's *calendar*, filled with all of our upcoming divine appointments. But we can be sure of this: God notices the purity of our preparation. We get His attention when we, like David, are faithful in our obscurity. His eyes focus on us when we are faithful, when no one else is watching. He is on a never-ending search for hearts like that. God-ordained opportunities can be expected when we are diligent in the dark. Giants will fall before those with a pure heart.

CHECK ENGINE LIGHTS

I have a strange relationship with my car's check engine light. It has promised to warn me when something is wrong. I have promised that I will ignore it as long as it is possible to do so. I hate check engine lights. You are driving along, things are going great, and then it suddenly appears. The light silently screams, *Things are not as good as you think they are....Something is not right.... This is going to cost you.* I think I would pay extra for a car without a check engine light! It is never a good feeling to discover that although things seem to be right, something is very wrong.

A few years ago, a *check engine light* came on inside my heart. Actually, it may have been on for years, but I refused to acknowledge its presence. Thankfully, during a season when I was desperately seeking God about my future, I became aware that *something* was wrong. On the outside, my life was going fairly well, but on the inside, there was a lack of peace. In desperation, I spent a few weeks praying and reading about issues of the heart. The soul-level honesty of those days was painful but necessary. The process was agonizing and often invasive, requiring a myriad of inside transformation. The hidden caverns of my unchecked heart ran deep. Eventually, God purified my heart and the *check engine light* disappeared.

THE MOST DECEITFUL THING

When I was a youth pastor, I once found myself in a counseling session with a distraught mother and her rebellious teenage son. He sat in stoic silence as she methodically listed his horrible exploits. Each time she described something he had done, she closed the story by reaching over and patting her son on the chest. With tears in her eyes, she'd say, "He has done these things, but he has such a good heart."

After hearing this a dozen times or more, I finally interrupted her. "You're wrong," I told her. "He does *not* have a good heart. His heart is actually the problem." I quoted Jeremiah 17:9 to her: *"The human heart is the most deceitful of all things, and desperately wicked. Who really knows how bad it is?"* I looked at her son and told him that if he would let God enter his rebellious heart, his life would turn around. We then dove underneath the murky surface of *what* he had done and started to deal with *why* he did it. We entered the realm of his heart, the place where real change can happen. His *check engine light* had been on for a long time and his own mom was helping him ignore it.

GOD WILL NOT SEND YOU ON A TRIP TO HIS *DIVINE INTENTIONS* FOR YOU WHILE A *CHECK ENGINE LIGHT* IS SHINING ON THE DASHBOARD OF YOUR HEART.

If you want to live in harmony with the assertions of this book, then you must be ready to deal with your heart. God will not send you on a long *road trip* that takes you to His *divine intentions* for you while a *check engine light* is shining on the dashboard of your heart. When the heart is wrong, nothing can be right. In fact, it's possible to be deceived by your own heart. As the prophet said, the heart *"is the most deceitful of all things."* Since it's driven by emotions, it's not a trustworthy guide. The purpose of our heart's *check engine light* is to make us aware of our motives, which hide in the deep, dark caves of our heart. This, of course, is a work of the Holy Spirit because only the Spirit can reveal what is in our hearts.

Later in his life, a repentant David cried out to God, *"Behold, you delight in truth in the inward being, and you teach me wisdom in the secret heart"* (Psalm 51:6 ESV). Look at the revealing language in this verse; David speaks of an *inward being* and a *secret heart*. God wants truth in the hidden places of your soul, where motive and intent live. This is so important to God because if we can get our motives, or the *why*, right, His plans—the *what*—will reveal themselves. Motives either fuel or halt destinies.

IF WE CAN GET OUR MOTIVES, OR THE *WHY*,
RIGHT, GOD'S PLANS—THE *WHAT*—
WILL REVEAL THEMSELVES.
MOTIVES EITHER FUEL OR HALT DESTINIES.

What does God want me to do with my life? What is my calling? What is the assignment God has for me? These are the wrong questions. We want *information* while God is focused on our *motivation*. We are worried about our *lives*, but God is concerned about our *hearts*.

If you allow God to purify your heart, there is no limit to the life He can offer you. The good news is, God is always ready and willing to do *heart surgery* on us! God makes this promise, *"I will give you a new heart, and I will put a new spirit in you. I will take out your stony, stubborn heart and give you a tender, responsive heart"* (Ezekiel 36:26). Your fresh start begins with a new heart.

"THEY SHALL SEE GOD"

There are almost endless promises in the Bible about what God will do for those who have a pure heart. I love all of them, but my favorite must be Matthew 5:8, which is found in Jesus's masterpiece teaching, the Sermon on the Mount. Among an amazing list of what it means to live a blessed life in the Beatitudes portion of that sermon, Jesus includes, "*Blessed are the pure in heart, for they shall see God*" (Matthew 5:8 NKJV). For many years, I have been intrigued by the last words of that verse: "*they shall see God.*" What does this mean? I certainly believe He is saying that purity of heart leads to a bigger revelation of God. But I am not convinced that Jesus was just talking about *vision*; I think He was also talking about *presence*. I believe Jesus was telling us that the *pure in heart* get to be in God's presence more often than those whose hearts are impure. Let me explain.

Not long ago, I became sick and told Jeanne that I needed to see a doctor. She didn't open her computer and show me photos of doctors. That would have been uncaring and unnecessary. Instead, she called a doctor and made me an appointment so I could *see* him. When I arrived at his office, I was in his physical presence, so I could take advantage of his help and regain my health. This is what Jesus is offering in Matthew 5:8. The *pure in heart* certainly have their *spiritual eyes* opened wider so they have a better *vision* of who God is. But that's only half of the promise. The pure in heart also get to experience a deeper level of God's presence. They have regular appointments with the King of the universe. They get to *see* God!

NO PAIN IS SO GREAT THAT JESUS CANNOT HEAL IT.

Seeing God changes everything. There is healing in His presence. No pain is so great that Jesus cannot heal it. When you are in His presence, all that was impossible becomes possible. When purity opens a door to His presence, other doors start opening, too. Divine appointments with God supernaturally create divine appointments with man. When you have been in His presence, His favor supports you and promotes you.

I see the relationship between *purity of heart* and *seeing God* like the relationship I have with my glasses. I need them to see. Without my glasses, life is blurry. I could not fulfill my calling because I need my glasses to write sermons and books. I need them to see the screen on my phone so I can follow up on the relational connections that fill my schedule. I need my glasses to drive to the airport and the other places where God has set up divine appointments for me. Without my glasses, I would have a difficult time living the life God intended for me to live. The analogy is not perfect, but you get the point. Purity of heart has a magnification effect. It causes God's plan to come into focus, giving you the vision you need to live out your purpose.

GUARD YOUR WELLSPRING

If you ever wanted to create a civilization in the wilderness, the first thing you would need is a water source. It could be a river or a lake, but the best water source would be a wellspring or fountainhead. This is an inexhaustible source of clean water that springs up from an underground aquifer. Wherever you find one of these, you will find abundant life. Once you find a water source like this, you can begin building your future. You can plant and harvest. Like an oasis in the desert, the wellspring will provide life even if you are surrounded by death. These springs are wonderful...but they are not indestructible. You have to guard them at all costs. If you lose your wellspring, you will eventually lose everything.

There's a verse in Proverbs that applies this *wellspring truth* to our hearts: "*Watch over your heart with all diligence, for from it flow the springs of life*" (Proverbs 4:23 AMP). Another translation says, "*Above all else, guard your heart, for everything you do flows from it*" (NIV). The *New Living Translation* says the heart "*determines the course of your life.*" According to the Bible, the condition of your heart affects "*everything you do.*" If your heart is in jeopardy, your life is in danger. But if your heart is right, your life will be productive. There is nothing more important than the condition of your heart.

Taking my *create a civilization in the wilderness* analogy a step further, imagine that things are humming along in your new society. Your wellspring is flowing and your world is growing. Everything is perfect...until tragedy strikes. You taste the water and something is wrong—it looks murky and burns your tongue a little. What once was pure has become tainted and is starting to make people sick. No matter how marvelous your civilization has become, all of your progress is now threatened. Unless you can purify the water, all of your dreams will disappear. This imaginary scenario is a reality for many civilizations. They run into trouble when their water sources are impure.

What is true of wellsprings is also true of hearts. Unless the *source* is pure, all that flows from it will be poisoned. It is impossible to build a great life with a bad heart.

NO WORK-AROUND FOR AN IMPURE HEART

There have been times when I tried to *work around* the impurities of my heart. I attempted to build my world while my source of life was tainted. All of us are capable of this type of self-deception, which just sets us up for failure and disappointment.

I'd like to illustrate this truth by sharing a rather vulnerable personal story: as I mentioned earlier, a few years ago, God was preparing me for a ministry change. He called me to go back to full-time traveling and speaking. But I could sense a caution from the Lord. The *check engine light* in my heart was shining bright. I was praying about it all the time, but I could not figure out what was wrong. Finally, God prompted me to read some devotional material on motives and being pure in heart. I knew my motives were off, but I still could not pinpoint exactly how my heart was impure. I needed God to reveal the hidden blockage in my heart and save me from myself.

One Wednesday afternoon, my layers of self-denial came crashing through. I had just finished writing a sermon for that Sunday. There were a bunch of opened books and research papers on my desk, surrounding my computer screen. I thought I would show the social media universe my strategic mess and tell them how excited I was for what God had given me to share on Sunday. So, I began taking pictures of the scene before me. I am embarrassed to say that I even walked over to my bookshelf and grabbed a few more books. I guess I wanted to make the desk look even fuller, to make myself look even smarter. I staged the desk and set it up for the perfect shot. I took a few photos and then edited them to perfection. I was about to post my glorious work on Facebook when I sensed the Holy Spirit speaking to my heart. He only said one word.

"*See.*"

Suddenly, the eyes of my heart were opened I *did see* what I was doing. I had just spent ten minutes setting up and even falsifying a photo I was about to send out for the world to admire. My motive was to look good and make people think I was awesome. I did not want to glorify God—I wanted to glorify me. With one three-letter word, God put the condition of my impure heart on display.

See!

GOD'S BLESSINGS ARE RESERVED FOR HIS PURPOSES AND HIS PROMOTIONS ARE FOR THOSE WHO LET HIM PURIFY THEIR HEARTS.

My heart was not ready for where God wanted to take me. My *well-spring* was contaminated and nothing could proceed until it was purified. On the outside, I had a mission to lift Him up, but on the inside, I wanted to lift myself up. God revealed to me that although my *mission* in life was pure, my *motives* were not. He showed me an ugly side of myself, an insecurity-driven self-promotion that I had never faced. Over the next two years, God unmasked and purified my false representations of myself. He corrected my motives. He lovingly walked with me through the hidden places of my heart and prepared me for my future. God had to extract my poisoned agenda before He could use me. The process was excruciating... but necessary. There was healing in the revealing. My heart was making me sick and it was showing up in my life. God showed me what was wrong so He could heal me.

God will not take you to a place He has not prepared you to go. He will not sustain what is impure. His blessings are reserved for His purposes and His promotions are for those who let Him purify their hearts.

Does God want to take you to a place where your heart is not prepared to go? Are you trying to build a great future with a bad heart? Is your *wellspring* fueling your future—or keeping you from it? If the latter, reach out to the only One who can purify your heart. You can start by praying, as David did:

Create in me a pure heart, O God, and renew a steadfast spirit within me. Do not cast me from your presence or take your Holy Spirit from me. Restore to me the joy of your salvation and grant me a willing spirit, to sustain me. (Psalm 51:10–12 NIV)

God loves to clean up what is wrong so He can reveal what the soul knows is right. His pathways are always pure. It is the application of His purity that sets the potential of your success. This is why your heart longs for His grace and why the *becoming* will lead to the *doing*.

I pray that this book has started your own healing process and your heart becomes so transformed that it carries you into all that God has for you. I pray for *pure promotions* in your life. I pray that you become the person God knows you to be so you can have the life He intends you to live.

DISCOVERY QUESTIONS

What *check engine lights* have you felt in your heart?

_____

_____

_____

_____

What are some corrections you need to make regarding your motives?

_____

_____

_____

_____

Why is guarding your heart so important?

_____

_____

_____

_____

Where does God want to take you that your heart is not prepared to go?

_____

_____

_____

_____

ABOUT THE AUTHOR

Doug K. Reed is a full-time writer and speaker who travels to conferences and churches both in the U.S. and internationally. He is the president of Partnership International, a non-profit organization dedicated to completing meaningful mission projects in some of the world's poorest environments. Partnership International has hosted thousands of people on short-term mission trips with a goal of sharing the love of Jesus with the neediest among us.

Doug also has more than thirty years of ministry experience and has served in several positions in the local church, including lead pastor. He is currently a teaching pastor at four churches in Kansas City, Missouri; Chester, Virginia; Troy, Missouri; and Helena, Montana.

He and his wife, Jeanne, and their youngest daughter, Jenna, reside in Lee's Summit, Missouri.

For more information about Partnership International, visit pitrips. com.